Fishing With
Marine Electronics

Fishing With Marine Electronics

Complete Angler's Library ®
North American Fishing Club
Minneapolis, Minnesota

Fishing With Marine Electronics

Copyright © 1992, North American Fishing Club

Library of Congress Catalog Card Number 92-81043
ISBN 0-914697-47-1

Printed in U.S.A.
    3   4   5   6   7   8   9

Contents

Acknowledgments

The North American Fishing Club would like to thank all those who have helped make this book a reality.

Wildlife artist Virgil Beck created the cover art. Artist David Rottinghaus provided all illustrations. Photos, in addition to the authors', were provided by Alumacraft, Joel Arrington, Joe Bucher, Soc Clay, Paul DeMarchi, Tom Huggler, Humminbird, Interphase, Bud Journey, Complete Angler's Library Managing Editor Ron Larsen, Lowrance Electronics, Magellan, Mercury Marine, Offshore Services (of Manasquan, New Jersey), Gary Parsons, *North American Fisherman* Editor Steve Pennaz, Thayne Smith, Toad Smith, Mark Strand, Allan Tarvid, Tennessee Wildlife Resources Agency and Vexilar.

And, a special thanks goes to the NAFC's publication staff for all their efforts: Publisher Mark LaBarbera, *North American Fisherman* Editor Steve Pennaz, Managing Editor of Books Ron Larsen, Associate Editor of Books Colleen Ferguson, Editorial Assistant of Books Mary Petrie-Terry and Art Director Dean Peters. Thanks also to Vice President of Product Marketing Mike Vail, Marketing Manager Cal Franklin and Marketing Project Coordinator Laura Resnik.

About The Authors

Kurt Beckstrom learned the art of fishing while pursuing crappies and bullheads on the small lakes and streams near his rural hometown in southern Minnesota. Much of his spare time was spent on the Straight River, or at the local gravel pit in search of fish to catch. A hook, worm and bobber were the simple beginnings of a lifelong devotion to the sport of fishing. Later, he'd work for area farmers baling hay or milking cows to earn money for more and better tackle.

Since then, Kurt's fishing experience has been varied; he has fished many species from coast to coast and in several Canadian provinces.

Nowadays, in addition to wetting a line where- and whenever possible, he spends a lot of time introducing his 5- and 3-year-old sons to the joys of fishing. "Both are enthusiastic young anglers," he says. "They don't need much encouragement from me."

Kurt also says he's one of the luckiest people around. First, because he works in the publishing industry as an Associate Editor for *North American Fisherman*. "I've wanted to be a writer since the seventh grade," he says. "I couldn't imagine doing anything else for a living."

His second love is the outdoors, especially sportfishing. Combining his two favorite activities is a dream come true, he adds.

Kurt earned a bachelor of science degree in agricultural and natural resources communications from Michigan State University in 1981. While attending MSU, he met his wife, Elaine. A farmer's daughter, she had a natural affection for the outdoors. However, she wasn't a dyed-in-the-wool angler, which Kurt admits made him wonder whether the relationship would last.

One day, after listening to a bit of salesmanship on the merits of fishing, she agreed to accompany him to the St. Joseph River. Within the first hour, she hooked, fought and landed a 13½-pound hen steelhead. The astonishment of being so soundly outfished in less than 60 minutes by a novice lasted only a short time. It was replaced by a certain belief that he had just witnessed the conversion of a non-angler into a lifelong fishing partner— the fun was just beginning in the Beckstrom family.

Before editing for *North American Fisherman*, Kurt worked extensively as an agricultural editor, writer and photographer—always, he says, toting a fishing rod on every assignment (just in case there was a chance to do what he likes best).

Buck Taylor is generally accepted among fishermen, editors and industry veterans as America's leading expert on fishing with depthfinders. As a journalist, he has the rare ability to take the many complexities of sonar use and present them with both candor and humor in an easy-to-digest way. As an active member of the Outdoor Writers Association of America, his reputation for honesty and integrity in his material has produced a constant demand for his work.

Writing about depthfinders since the 1970s, Taylor's expertise has earned the respect of anglers worldwide and won numerous awards for excellence among his peers in professional journalism. To a large degree, it probably was Buck's ground-breaking articles and his first book on depthfinders which earned for him the honor of being included in *Living Legends Of American Sportfishing* by Larry Colombo. Colombo's book details achievements of the 100 men and women who have contributed the most to sportfishing as we know it today.

A full-time freelance writer specializing in outdoor subjects, Buck Taylor has been sharing his knowledge and experience with readers in American sporting publications for over 20 years. His

personal success story is unique. He graduated from Florida State University with an accounting major and worked in that field for many years before deciding to quit the business routine and work at something he really loved: the outdoors. With no background in either journalism or photography, Taylor used sheer determination and personal integrity to carve out a place for himself among outdoor writers. His first book on sonar was *The Complete Guide To Using Depthfinders*, which he self-published in 1981.

A true Southern gentleman by birth and heritage, Taylor has traveled to Africa, Central and South America, Europe and all across North America in search of photographs and materials for his books and articles on fishing and hunting. His style of writing backed with years of factual experience has taken many readers on delightful journeys in search of angling and hunting adventures. In addition to his career as a writer, Taylor also works as a professional wildlife habitat and fisheries management consultant. He lives on an 850-acre farm in rural south Alabama. When not traveling, he combines work with pleasure by hunting, fishing, trapping and photographing wildlife.

Foreword

Understanding how to properly install, operate and interpret your sonar will help you catch more fish. That's why we've added *Fishing With Marine Electronics* to the NAFC's popular Complete Angler's Library. For those of you who have read the owner's manual that accompanied your unit, this book will be a real treat. It will help explain many of the complicated topics discussed, and lay the foundation you need to get the most out of the sophisticated piece of equipment resting in your boat.

Most of today's anglers know that modern sonar not only shows you how deep you are fishing, but also whether the lake bottom is hard or soft, if you're over fish (and their size), where the thermocline is located, and many other things. Sonar can also be used for such specific tasks as tracking downrigger balls and tailoring presentations for lethargic winter fish. There are even sonar units that locate fish hiding in shoreline cover or suspending at boatside.

The fact that modern sonar can do all these great things is moot, however, if you don't know how to make your unit perform at its peak. Fortunately, you don't have to be a rocket scientist to get the most out of your sonar, especially after you are able to grasp the basics.

Our goal for writing *Fishing With Marine Electronics* was not to make operating your sonar more complicated, but to simplify some difficult concepts and help you understand what all those little buttons on your unit do. To do that, we'll cover several important topics: the history of sonar and why it was developed; how sonar works; how to install the transducer; the proper way to operate various sonar units; how to interpret sonar signals; and how to use sonar to locate bass, crappies, stripers, walleyes, pike and muskies and trout and salmon throughout the seasons.

The first, and undoubtedly most important, step in getting the most out of your sonar is installing it properly. Modern sonar units are well-built technological marvels that inform you about the mysterious world beneath your boat—information you can use to find and catch fish. If you're having problems with your sonar unit, it is most likely because of the way the unit was installed, not the unit itself. That's why we have dedicated an entire chapter to this important topic.

According to the co-authors, sonar expert Buck Taylor and NAFC Associate Editor Kurt Beckstrom, many sonar problems can be avoided by taking the time to review the owner's manual and following the installation instructions provided.

Knowing what to look for while reviewing the data displayed on your sonar screen is the key to unlocking the information it is providing. In this book we'll cover the entire range of depth-finders, including flashers, chart recorders, liquid crystals and video units. All of these units are based on the same sonar principles, differing only in the ways they process and display the information they receive via the transducer. (While flashers have a dubious future as many of the major manufacturers have dropped them from their product lines, there are still many anglers who rely on them. I'm one of them. In this book, you'll find everything you need to know about operating and interpreting their signals.)

We'll take you onto the water to explain the many ways sonar will help you catch more fish. For example, we'll discuss how sonar can help you eliminate the unproductive water and concentrate your efforts in areas that hold fish. The old saying that 10 percent of the water holds 90 percent of the fish is often true, especially when you're fishing bass, walleyes, crappies and other species that tend to school. Find one, and others will follow. Sonar will help locate that all-important first fish.

Finally, we'll step into the world of navigation with marine electronic equipment. An entire chapter is devoted to Long Range Navigation (loran technology) and the Global Positioning System (GPS). We discuss how each system works and the advantages and disadvantages that are inherent in each.

GPS is a much promoted technology, and rightfully so. This chapter gives you an inside look at it, as anglers everywhere realize its advantages.

I hope you enjoy and learn from *Fishing With Marine Electronics*. We're proud of this addition to the NAFC's popular Complete Angler's Library.

Steve Pennaz
Executive Director
North American Fishing Club

Understanding Sonar

1

How Sonar Developed Into Fishing Gear

With the roar of the big boat's outboard subsiding, the angler continues to ease back on the throttle, some 100 yards away from the submerged stump field. He had discovered the drowned stumps on the video display unit shortly after launching his craft a quarter-mile down the shoreline. Once again, he silently thanks the genius who designed the tiny hull-mounted television camera that could penetrate up to 800 yards in even the inkiest water.

His solar-powered trolling motor pulls the rig, almost noiselessly, toward the shallows, as he switches his bow-mounted video unit to the audible mode. If he hadn't seen the fish on the screen, finning lazily among a tangle of roots, the voice that crackled from the unit would have drawn his attention to it. He had programmed the machine to speak up only when it looked in on a bass of 3 pounds, or more.

A second later, a faint red dot appears on the screen in the relative position of a point approximately 6 inches above and the same distance in front of, the bass' nose. The angler quickly scans the water's surface for a spot of light, the end of an otherwise invisible laser beam, emanating from a mast mounted at the boat's stern. This will be the aim-point for his cast. On the cast, a minnow-imitating lure, with the line-tie at the tail instead of the head, enters the water near the red spot, well within the 3-foot diameter "forgiveness zone."

In a heartbeat, a miniaturized homing device installed within

Stringers like this were instrumental in convincing skeptical fishermen that using sonar in sportfishing was not a fad, and that sonar was here to stay.

How Sonar Developed Into Fishing Gear   13

the lure's nose locates the underwater beam coming from the television camera, and silently glides down the electronic path toward the fish. It doesn't reach the end of the path—which would have triggered a "stall-and-shimmy" action—before the 3¼-pounder launches its attack. It's technology borrowed from the military's laser-guided "smart bomb."

Even for modern NAFC Members, who are among the most up-to-date anglers around, this scenario probably seems a little hard to believe. But is it? Probably not. Just think back to your grandfather's time. After 15 years on his favorite lake, he found (by accident) that deep-water hump where he was able to pick up a bass or two, or maybe a few crappies whenever he returned to it (if he was able to locate the spot again).

Do you think that, while sitting with him in his 12-foot wooden rowboat, you could have convinced him that someday an angler with a good hydro map and an electronic depthfinder would be able to find the same spot in approximately 15 minutes? And still return to that exact same spot time and time again? Probably not!

Even in the 1930s, when sonar was in its infancy, only a handful of scientists, and perhaps a few of the military experts for whom they worked, could imagine the incredible impact that their years of experimentation and refinements would have in our modern world. You can bet the rent money that probably none of them ever envisioned that operation of a sonar unit would someday become second-nature to a sportfisherman, almost as much as baiting a hook. After all, they were preparing men and machines for a life-and-death struggle in which thousands of lives and millions of tons of cargo, both military and civilian, were on the line (a struggle they had hoped would never come. But, it did).

Sonar (SOund NAvigation Ranging) technology was still in swaddling clothes before World War II. The German Navy, during the first World War, had given the Americans and British a taste of what submarine warfare would be like. In return, England and America began to develop sonar as a tool of defense. American researchers lost interest in sonar after the Kaiser was defeated; however, the British persevered. British scientists knew that the established shipping lanes to the United States would be their lifeline if another war of that magnitude broke out. The only way to keep these lanes clear of enemy submarines was to develop reliable ways of finding the submarines before they could attack surface vessels.

By 1939, England's Royal Navy had about 160 sonar-equipped destroyers, while the American Navy had only 60, or so. While it was then top-of-the-line equipment, by present-day standards, it was very primitive. Before Hitler's U-boats began to heat things up in the Atlantic, the technology was used mainly for navigational purposes—locating buoys, defining shipping channels or determining overall water depth.

This was really second-generation technology. The first generation was the simple listening devices that could determine the direction of sounds from another vessel's propellers. However, this "passive" sonar could not provide enough information for the operator to calculate the other vessel's range, speed or direction of travel—all of which were essential for ensuring a destroyer crew's continued good health. Ironically, modern sonar operators consider the current, highly sophisticated passive sonar to be the best mode of detection because it lets a ship's operator gather a considerable amount of information about another vessel without alerting the other ship to its presence.

During the World War II era, however, active sonar was believed to be the electronics of the future. The control panel and information processing unit were big and cumbersome, and the transducer was mounted inside a retractable dome on the ship's hull. It worked just like modern units do; electrical energy was sent to the transducer which was then converted into sound energy. Most sound waves that went out were lost forever. A few of the signals that did bounce off a submarine were picked up on the return trip by the ship's receiver. Considering such factors as water temperature and density, a skilled sonar operator could calculate the location of the "enemy" sub.

In order to search a specified section of water, early transducers had to be rotated, and sound waves were fired and received at precise points along the "sweep." This "searchlight" method was time-consuming; however, the most limiting factor was that the system's maximum range was only a few thousand yards—practically within your back pocket when compared to the ocean's vastness. A submarine could be within torpedo range before being discovered by the targeted ship.

Needless to say, when Hitler turned loose his submarines in

the Atlantic, it became almost a turkey-shoot for the U-boats. A dozen or so U-boats, operating off North America's eastern seaboard from Newfoundland to Florida, in the Gulf of Mexico and in waters off northern South America, destroyed ships, mostly civilian trading vessels, with impunity. Nearly 300 ships were attacked during the eight months following the day the United States and Germany swapped declarations of war. U-boat attacks occurred all across the Atlantic, but, by far, the majority of them were aimed at ships of various countries that were bound for American ports. Some German U-boat skippers became so brazen that they launched daytime attacks against ships in full view of seaside resort-goers. At the time, there wasn't much the United States could do to defend its coastline because of its lack of more sonar equipment and the trained operators to run it.

With today's advanced technology and properly trained operators, it is easy to detect ships that are miles away. Researchers' discovery of what's known as the "bell effect," in which sound waves in water converge and collide many times, gaining acceleration so they can travel for miles, and the advent of more advanced, high-powered transmitters, enable modern military sonar operators to pinpoint submarines at great distances.

Sonar In Peacetime

Following World War II, companies that had once built sonar equipment for the military were free to seek new markets. However, the units were bulky and expensive so those markets were fairly limited. Certainly, they did not include the owners of sportfishing craft. Commercial fishermen were fair game, however, because their boats were large enough to accommodate such cumbersome equipment and they could realize increased profit by being able to quickly and accurately locate large schools of fish.

Although it was some time in coming, the next step was into the sportfishing industry. It was taken by a Midwestern trucking and produce businessman named Carl Lowrance and his sons, Darrell and Arlen. In the 1950s, all three had become superior anglers as a result of their shared interest in scuba diving. They knew more about fish movement and behavior than a lot of anglers would ever know. Then, in 1956, when the Lowrances traveled to Canada to fish the country's cold, deep waters for trophy lake trout, Carl hit upon an idea that would, if successful, turn

Darrell Lowrance poses with the millionth ''little green box'' produced by his company. This particular milestone in sonar electronics history was achieved in 1983.

How Sonar Developed Into Fishing Gear 17

even the most ordinary fisherman into an expert.

The idea arose when the Lowrances went fishing with a guide whose boat was equipped with a World War II-vintage sonar unit. It operated at 50 kilohertz (kHz)—the standard frequency of the day—and was good mainly for reading water depth and determining bottom structure. Occasionally, if a school of fish was large enough, the school would show up on the display screen; however, it wouldn't show individual fish. "We discussed that shortcoming, and the possibilities of making a unit that would isolate fish on the screen," Darrell Lowrance recalls.

Still, that guide's sonar proved invaluable. With the lake trout holding tight to the bottom in 60 to 100 feet of water, the normal practice of trolling lead-core or wire line produced minimal results. That old sonar unit, however, led the anglers to a hotspot that produced twice as many fish in a day as most anglers would catch in a week. The hotspot was a submerged hump that, without the use of sonar, would have remained undetected. Years of observing fish underwater paid off for the Lowrances. Even though the electronic marvel they were using did not indicate a single fish, the anglers knew from previous experience that the hump just might hold lake trout. With the boat positioned over the hump, they began casting weighted lures to the deep edges. The trout took the offerings as they were retrieved up the slope.

"The trout created quite a stir at camp when we came in," remembers Carl. "Everyone wanted to know our secret. But, it wasn't really a secret. We had simply taken our knowledge of the different habits of fish and used the old sonar to find the most likely habitat."

The First Portable Sonar

At home later that summer, Carl and his sons began what turned out to be a period of extensive research into the world of sonar technology. They had collected all the information they could about the use of sonar for ocean depth soundings. Soon they discovered that a sound wave at a frequency of 50 kHz was too long for sportfishing purposes. The pulse length is just too long for the unit to capture the image of individual fish. While perfect for penetrating ocean depths, low-frequency sound waves tended to meld objects that were, in reality, several feet apart. This created a blob on the display screen.

Sound Wave Pulse Length

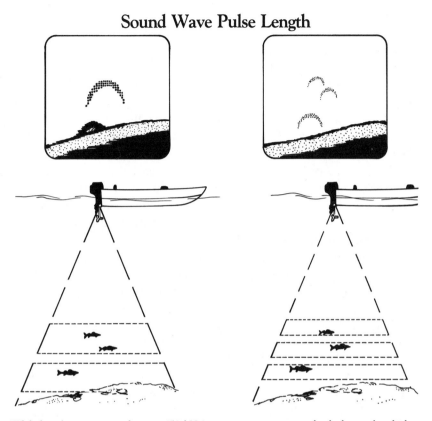

While low-frequency sound waves (50 kHz) can penetrate extreme depths better than high-frequency waves, their long pulse lengths tend to blend the signal of objects close to one another. The Lowrances developed a unit that produced short bursts of sound waves (200 kHz), which allowed anglers to actually see individual fish.

Their solution was to boost the frequency to 200 kHz. With the shorter pulse lengths, the unit could distinguish fish from each other and from the bottom itself, as long as there was at least six inches of space between them.

Unit size was the next obstacle. At the time, fishing boats were generally small, open "rowboats," powered by equally small outboards (just kicker motors by modern standards). What's more, these boats had no electrical system, no wiring, no circuit breakers—nothing. Obviously, then, the Lowrance's sonar unit would have to be small, lightweight and able to work on the amount of power a pair of dry cell batteries could provide.

At the same time, the electronics industry was undergoing a revolution—one that would make the Lowrance's dream a reality. Tiny transistors that rendered big, clumsy vacuum tubes obsolete were just hitting the market. Miniaturization had arrived and the Lowrances took advantage of it.

Carl and his sons took their ideas and designs to a small West Coast manufacturer with experience in building sonar units. There, the first limited quantity of high-frequency, transistorized "flashers" was produced. But, the housing—a blue fiberglass box—just couldn't stand up to the rigors of shipping. And, many "blue boxes," and the sensitive electronics within, were damaged during shipment. Darrell Lowrance said another problem was "frequency drift," in which the units could not maintain a particular frequency. This resulted in indiscriminate and undesirable flashes appearing on the dial, he explained.

The contract was given to a second, larger manufacturer who built about 700 boxes (gray this time). Unfortunately, they weren't any better than the first generation. Not only did the cases fail to protect the delicate instrumentation, but the electronic parts in many units also were inferior. Many units just didn't work when turned on. Plagued by quality-control problems, the Lowrances decided to "do it ourselves."

In 1959, they began building what veteran anglers remember as the "red box"—the first working sonar built exclusively for fishermen. This time, the cases were made of steel—heavy, but nearly indestructible. Carl and his sons spent many long days and nights in the shop, producing units not only for sale but to replace nonfunctioning earlier models. "We worked seven days a week at the factory," recalls Darrell.

By November 1959, the unit's outward appearance had changed once again. Steel housings were replaced by aluminum, and the color had changed from red to green.

The Little Green Box

In time, the Lowrances finally produced their dream machine. It was dubbed the Lowrance LFP-300; however, more than one generation of anglers will remember it as "the little green box." During its 25-year lifespan, more than a million units slid off the conveyer. In all, there were six versions, ending with the LFP-300E (denoting the sixth upgrade of the unit's electronics).

In 1959, however, a lot of "selling" was required to convince anglers of its merits. Carl Lowrance, the infant depthfinder company's designated public relations man, traveled the country talking to anglers, fishing guides, owners of sporting goods stores, out-door writers and anyone else who would listen about the "green box." Not only would he talk, but he would *show* them how it worked.

Thayne Smith, author of *North American Fisherman's* "Boats & Accessories" column, was one of the early converts. He was writing an outdoor column for several Midwestern newspapers at the time. "One day Carl called me up and said he wanted to show me his new fishfinder," Smith said. "I was to meet him at the air-port the next day, boat in tow, and take him to any local lake of my choosing—preferably one that had a reputation of being 'fished out.' Back then, if a fisherman experienced poor success on a particular body of water, the standard excuse was that the lake was fished out.

"Carl showed me, however, that the lake I chose was anything *but* dead. Man, did we catch fish, mostly crappies and bass. Before he got back on the plane, he gave the box to me. I still have it today." Smith must have been thoroughly convinced as he later worked for Lowrance Electronics as a public relations writer.

Still, general resistance among those early anglers remained strong. Many just didn't believe it could work; others considered it just another gimmick. Worse than that, they thought it was a gimmick with a $150 price tag.

Things changed for the better when Carl captured the atten-tion of a few "Grand Fishing Masters," including Ted Trueblood, Homer Circle and Erwin Bauer. Their rave reviews in national sporting publications put the green box on the map. The favor-able publicity, followed by an all-out campaign to educate anglers in big fishing states like Minnesota, Wisconsin and Illinois, fi-nally made the project a success. "We hired six people to spend their summers in the Northern states, just demonstrating the so-nar," said Darrell.

Throughout the 1960s, '70s and '80s, many other sonar com-panies introduced their own lines of fine sonar products. After the flasher came the paper graph. This unit actually burned marks onto heat-sensitive paper that scrolled beneath the "pen." These marks represented the bottom contour, baitfish or gamefish.

In 1969, Vexilar introduced the first recognized paper graph specifically designed for sportfishing. The 155 was initially devel-oped for the exploding Great Lakes salmon fishery—particularly

The next major step in sportfishing sonar technology was the development of the paper graph, or chart recorder. The Vexilar 155 was one of the first, providing a permanent record of bottom structure and fish location.

in Lake Michigan for the newly introduced chinook and coho salmon. It was another sportfishing opportunity, as well as a tool to reduce out-of-control alewife populations.

The graph's advantage was that the image on the paper was permanent. If the angler happened to glance away for a moment, or even needed a minute to reset a line, he could always see what his boat had passed over. If he missed seeing something the first time, chances are good that the object would still be in view when he returned his attention to the sonar.

Paper graphs were also much easier to read; the angler could interpret the graph's permanent marks more easily than a flasher dial's transitory blips.

The disadvantage to using a paper graph is that the paper must be changed from time to time. This is both time-consuming and expensive. Paper-graph technology was the mainstay for a number of years. A few modern anglers still consider it superior to other types of sonar. However, the liquid crystal graph, which you'll read more about in a later chapter, replaced the paper graph in most anglers' boats.

Liquid crystal graphs (LCGs) are now the most popular units on the market. Even though the display is not permanent, it remains on the screen long enough for an angler to obtain all the information, even if he's distracted for a few moments. Companies like Humminbird, Lowrance, Impulse, Interphase and others all quickly supported the new technology. Although the first models were not accepted easily by anglers, later versions with improved resolution won them over.

Some LCG features are three-dimensional-scanning and side-scanning units. The 3-D feature should provide the angler with a more distinct overall understanding of what lies below; however, many anglers remain skeptical. Side-scanning units, on the other hand, are extremely popular. Many fishermen who contributed information to this book agree that Bottom Line's SideFinders play an important role in their fishing success. The units (Scout and Stalker) scan the waters up to about 120 feet from the boat's side. Only fish that are 7 inches or larger show up on the screen.

It is amazing that there are so many high-quality electronic devices today to help anglers catch fish; however, one fact remains undisputed: The door that led to today's vast array of choices was opened by "the little green box."

2

Getting To Know Depthfinders

Having a depthfinder in your boat will not cause fish to jump over the sides and land in your livewell or ice chest. In addition, the act of turning on your unit will not automatically cause fish to gather in mass below the boat. Depthfinders do not create hunger pains in fish, either. As if these bothersome thoughts were not enough to make your wallet tremble while checking out the price tag on modern sonar gear, there is more.

A few American anglers still continue to catch fish without use of sonar equipment. In at least one extreme case, there is a bank executive who has been exposed to all the heavy-duty operational niceties of multiple-unit sonar gear, and he still insists he can catch as many, if not more, fish without depthfinders than most anglers using several units on their boats. (A point which he gleefully has proven on more than one occasion.)

However, this will be an attempt to justify the money you have spent, or are about to spend, on depthfinders. The use of sonar gear must be done with an eye for moderation. There is little cost-effectiveness in bolting a $1,200 graph unit on the bench seat of your 10-foot johnboat. The unit will be capable of performing a number of feats in underwater conditions that are unlikely to be experienced by typical johnboat users who rarely venture far from shore. However, you will be forced to pay for the numerous dials, knobs, whistles and gingerbread built into the expensive graph, even though you never use them.

Serious fishermen, like this angler taking a nice striper, are prepared for anything, and sonar equipment is no exception. They may be fishing the shallows one moment and searching deeper, open water the next.

Getting To Know Depthfinders

Matching sonar equipment to fishing conditions is only logical. If you enjoy capturing fillets in water of 30-foot depths or less, you will have a small need for units capable of drawing out ice-age remnants on the ocean floor. A simple flasher or liquid crystal unit with a 50-foot scale will do nicely.

Conversely, if you love fishing for big salmon that cruise deep, open waters in the Great Lakes, you will need a more sophisticated sonar tool, or perhaps, several of them. When the bottom depth exceeds the maximum depth shown on the depthfinder scale, funny things happen. On a graph, you simply watch the bottom disappear from sight on the paper, which is then drawn in at some imaginary point down around your shoelaces. When the bottom gets too deep for a flasher, it starts giving you fake readings; the bottom signals around the face of the dial continue to appear somewhere else which seems appropriate to the unit.

Deep-water sonar requirements can be met in a number of ways. You can purchase units with 100-foot or more depth scales. You can purchase a unit with multiple scales, allowing you to shift gears with the flick of a switch, transforming the depth readout from one set of numbers to another. In the event of an emergency (such as running over unexpected extreme water depths), you can watch the signals carefully on your flasher as they make a complete circle around the dial. If your flasher has a 60-foot depth scale and the water is 85 feet deep, the bottom reading on the unit will make a complete circle around the dial, pass "0" and stop at "25 feet" on the scale.

While this is all very logical to your sonar flasher, you must notice when the bottom reading sneaks past zero. Then, it becomes a simple matter to add the two figures together to find the correct bottom depth. If the flasher shows bottom at 25 feet after passing zero, you add the maximum depth on the dial (i.e. 30, 50 or 60 feet) to determine the actual depth under the boat. In the case of a 60-foot flasher, you would calculate bottom at 60 + 25, the sum of which is 85.

In the late 1960s, Chevrolet manufactured a series of big-block "muscle cars" whose giant 454 engines could be souped-up to produce an incredible 500 horsepower quite easily. Young and old people alike delighted in taking these cars to the local dragstrip on Sunday afternoons to race against all comers. During the competition, the drivers were faced with the same type of sit-

Using your depthfinder to discover a ditch or cut in shallows can produce excellent fishing. Make sure to be extremely quiet so that you don't spook the fish.

uation mentioned above (the speedometer needle passing the "maximum" speed and continuing on around to start again). As these engines would routinely exceed 120 mph in second gear, it was an every-weekend affair to watch the needle make a full circle, pass the blank area where there were no numbers and climb to 30 or 40 mph again. However, unlike fishermen using flashers, drivers rarely failed to recognize when this was taking place.

Depthfinders: How And Why They Work

Sonar units help fishermen fill stringers, win tournaments and keep their boats away from places hazardous to the health of props, lower units and fiberglass hulls. There are many depthfinder models on the market, and all work similarly using the principles of sonar. Unit features, quality and capabilities vary substantially, as do price tags. Yet below the cosmetics, there lies a pulsating heart of crystal which can be the most important tool in your boat when fish are difficult to find.

You do not have to understand complex formulas or graduate from technical school with honors to use sonar equipment properly. Nor is it required that you know each piece of circuitry within the unit by name and color code. If that were the case, few anglers would be using depthfinders.

Yet, the complex functions are all there to serve you. Some units have self-adjusting, practically "hands off" operation to compensate for water-depth changes. Others offer dual-frequency transducers that provide appropriate performance for both shallow- and deep-water use. Some models are linked to a Loran-C unit (more about loran in Chapter 17) providing coordinates printed out on chart paper.

Microprocessor circuitry produces space-age technology which allows you to examine only a "slice" or layer of the water at a time, or zoom the detail within a given sector into still larger, more detailed displays. These mini-computers have noise-reject features to block electrical interference and/or eliminate "cross talk" between two separate units running in the same boat. The really fancy ones can actually eliminate most of the surface clutter by varying the sensitivity level in the receiver for close (surface) signals and more distant (fish, structure) signals.

Video depthfinders, whether considered "fad" or "state of the art," are the industry's attempt to bridge the gap between flashers and graphs. They display images on a screen instead of burning them on paper. Some store the most-recent information for recall, and many can be stopped or "frozen" for study. With dual-angle transducers and dual-frequency transmitters, there is virtually no combination the average fisherman is likely to encounter that modern depthfinders cannot handle. What follows will be an explanation of the ways to *use* your depthfinder effectively, without being too technical.

Properly installed and operated, a good depthfinder will furnish a staggering amount of useful information for the person who takes time to learn how to read the signals. Indeed, there is an initial time period when serious study must be given to understanding sonar readout. You cannot simply bolt one of the things onto your boat and flip on the switch expecting the fun to mate-

This Bluewater Pro LFG-360 flasher from Lowrance is a good example of the added versatility of flashers with dual depth scales. It makes signal reading much easier.

rialize as if by magic. Learning takes time—lots of time. But, when it all falls into place, your success on the water is going to increase dramatically.

Many depthfinders have special features designed to assist in particular fishing procedures. Some, for example, are excellent for reading details in very deep water; others work more efficiently in shallow areas. Many graphs and flashers have selective depth scales built into their operational systems which allow a full range of detailed readout in various water depths. For the most part, it will depend upon your ability to understand what the unit is saying (not the fancy stuff the salesman promoted) that will put fillets on the supper table. After analyzing your sonar needs, you will be in a better position to evaluate the features offered on units you may view in the store.

Basics Of What Makes Them Work

Your sonar system has three fundamental parts. When electricity is added, they work together to generate the desired result: an image on a screen or dial which details shapes and objects in the water beneath your boat.

The transmitter. A small amount of current from your battery is taken by the transmitter and converted into pulses. These pulses are then fed to the transducer, which is in the water.

The transducer. As the pulses from the transmitter reach the transducer, they are modified, being completely changed from electrical impulses to sound impulses. These mechanical sound waves are then released into the water through the transducer "eye," or the center of its internal crystal.

Sound pulses in the water travel away from the transducer at just under 5,000 feet per second. When they strike an underwater object or bottom structure, they are reflected back up to the waiting transducer. Called "echoes," the reflected sound waves enter the transducer where they are then converted back into electrical impulses.

The receiver. The returning echoes, once converted back into electrical form, are run through an amplifier to make the impulse signal stronger. These impulses are then used to trigger display information on the depthfinder's dial or screen. In flasher and paper-graph units, a perfectly-synchronized, spinning wheel or belt beneath the dial directs these tiny bursts of electricity toward neon bulbs, or through the tip of a keen wire moving across the face of treated paper.

Flashers light up and graphs burn marks on paper with the returning electrical pulses. Video and liquid crystal units don't need belts or wheels because they merely display signals directly on the screen.

Because the speed of sound traveling through water is a constant, the depthfinder can give accurate readings of the distance to the object reflecting the signal, based upon the amount of time required for the pulse to make its roundtrip. The spinning wheel or belt revolves at exactly the speed necessary for it to be in the correct position on the depth scale when the returning signal is received, converted and fed to the bulb or stylus. Nowhere is the phrase "timing is everything" more appropriate than when applied to the inner workings of your depthfinder.

How Sonar Works

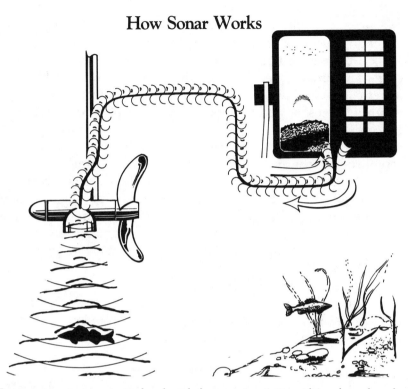

Battery current converts into pulses through the transmitter (upper right) and travels to the transducer in the water (mounted on trolling motor). The pulses are then changed from electrical to sound and released into the water (represented by dark lines moving to the lake's bottom). After they strike an object, the pattern reverses itself, bringing the pulses back to your unit's screen and showing you what's below the water.

You might look at the face of your unit and think the readings are continuous, especially at the "0" mark on the dial. Actually, your unit is sending out pulses one at a time. Each and every pulse must make its full trip before the next one starts. This is why the belt or wheel on your depthfinder slows noticeably when you change over to a deeper depth scale. The unit actually gears itself down to a pace slow enough to capture the returning pulse from the maximum depth on your scale before sending another one.

A typical sounding rate for flashers may be 24 times per second, while some specialty graphs may only send one every two seconds.

According to the experts, the particular type of power supplied to the depthfinders is not especially important. Almost all depthfinders today work on 12-volt DC, and the differences between wet-cell batteries and those with dry cells have little or no effect on performance. The wet-cell battery normally lasts a little longer, but depthfinders are designed to use only the amount of current required. You will not get more power to the unit by using a wet-cell over a dry-cell battery. In fact, you can operate the depthfinder just as well by wiring a pair of 6-volt lantern batteries in a series.

Your depthfinder should be connected to the boat's main battery if the alternative is connecting it to the trolling motor battery. The engine, while running, constantly recharges the main battery, providing a steady voltage level. The trolling motor battery does not get recharged, so current to the depthfinder weakens as the day progresses. (The depthfinder will not materially weaken the battery, but the trolling motor does it routinely in a matter of hours.)

Depthfinders actually draw very little current, but they need their juice at full-strength for maximum performance. If the battery cannot provide a full dose of energy to the depthfinder, it doesn't function as well.

Special Scales And Depth Readings

Should your fishing activities be confined to water that is 20 feet deep or less year-round, there is little need for multiple depth scales on your unit. Actually, you could select a unit providing maximum detail in the 0-to-20-foot depth range, and have everything you need for a sonar readout. However, if you should use that limited unit in water 50 or 100 feet deep, searching for stripers or salmon, for example, its signals would be almost impossible to read.

A depthfinder with a single, 50-foot depth scale will show bottom readings accurately at 65 feet (or any other reasonable depth). However, as mentioned earlier, the "bottom" reading will appear on the unit at 15 feet. Should you be searching this water for suspended fish holding at 10 or 20 feet, you would have a tough time trying to sort out fish signals from bottom signals on the dial. In this situation, selective depth scales are big medicine for fishermen. Flip the switch, and you can change the maximum depth reading to double or triple the original scale on the dial.

Incidentally, running over water 55 feet deep while watching a flasher depthfinder set on the 50-foot scale can be stressful, es-

Transducer Cone Angles

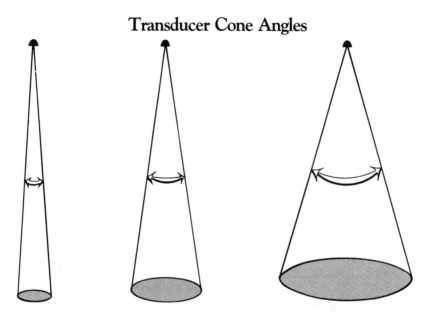

The cone angle degree represents how fast or slow the pulses spread. They can range from 8 degrees (left) to 16 degrees (middle) to 32 degrees (right). Some are wide enough to reach 50.

pecially if your boat is booming along at 50 or 60 mph!

When using paper graphs, it is often an advantage to use re-duced depth scales. And using the most shallow scale available to cover the water depth you are fishing, you get detail spread out over the entire width of the paper in maximum size. This provides the best possible overview of bottom conditions. When a partic-ular image merits an even closer look, the "zoom" mechanics can be used to enlarge it. One unit on the market today allows you to set the zoom water layer in 1-foot increments. With detail like that available on paper, you could easily distinguish Neptune from his mermaids.

Signal Cones

Sonar manufacturers offer a wide range of cone angles in their transducers. The cone angle basically translates into the shape of the sound pulses in the water after they leave your transducer. The pulses emanate from the eye of the transducer and spread in an ever-increasing circle as they move farther away. The "degree" of cone angle simply means how fast or how slow the pulses spread. (It's a rather complex, theoretical subject. One manufacturer explains it this way: The angle of the cone is a product of the inverse relationship between the diameter of the crystal and the energy which passes through it.)

Anyway, some cone angles are as tight as 8 degrees, while others are wide enough to form a 50-degree angle. The difference, in this case, in square footage of underwater real estate represented by the returning signals is quite substantial. A "wide" cone angle will show you the treetop and the fish playing cards next to it. A narrow cone-angle may only show you the red ace. Manufacturers are not likely to agree in describing the effects of their cone angles. The guy whose inverse whatchamacallit makes a tight cone says he has concentrated the power into a smaller area so his unit produces superior detail in that area of readout. Then, the other guy whose machine displays detail over a wider bottom area will counter by saying he gives you a better idea of what is really under the boat, instead of providing only a peek. In a way, both manufacturers are correct.

For comparison purposes, a transducer which spreads impulses in a 22-degree cone in 20 feet of water would produce readout detail over an 8-foot diameter area of the bottom. Another unit with an 8-degree cone would record activity reports over a 3-foot-diameter bottom circle at the same depth. Think about the differences between a floodlight and a spotlight, if the power source is constant. Which would you rather use if you're walking through a swamp filled with alligators?

Transducer Frequencies

Various sonar manufacturers individualize the frequencies of their units slightly, but most units fall in the range between 190 and 200 kHz for freshwater fishing use. Other common frequencies occur at either 50 or 150 kHz. Generally, the higher frequencies are best suited for freshwater angling where fine detail is important. Lower frequencies work better in salt and very deep water.

Superior detail-producing ability is called resolution. Some of the high-frequency kHz units on the market today can isolate (or separate) a fish holding only a few inches off the bottom. These same units can draw the water's thermocline layer on your graph paper because the sudden temperature change causes a change in water density. Such is the world of high-frequency units.

Unfortunately, nothing in this world is perfect. High-frequency

Because fine detail is important when fishing in freshwater, high-frequency units are quite popular. This paper graph utilizes 192 kHz while a technician charts true running depths of more than 200 lures.

sonar units do not perform well in extremely deep water. The signals are absorbed somewhat by the objects they strike. The problem is not major in most waters fished by freshwater anglers; but, saltwater captains who fish the briny depths probably wouldn't trade you a rusty hook for a dozen high-frequency units.

Portable Units

Several manufacturers presently offer units with bolt-on or suction-cup transducer mounts. These portable depthfinders normally are powered by self-contained batteries and are a favorite with many anglers who do not have their own boats. Portability is a great advantage to the fisherman on vacation who must rent a boat, or one who fishes upon occasion with a pal whose rig lacks sonar equipment.

Whiteline, Grayline Feature

Many quality graphs offer a feature which enables the operator to "lift" objects away from the bottom reading on the paper. The feature does not actually increase the distance between the bottom and nearby objects. It shades out the heavy bottom reading so that objects near it are less likely to blend. This makes it much easier to spot fish holding close to the bottom. Otherwise, these fish signals often tend to blend into the bottom reading and go unnoticed. Most good graph units on the market today offer this feature. It definitely is worth asking for when shopping.

Chart Paper Retainer

This feature has real advantages for the serious fisherman who saves his chart paper for future reference. Some graphs spew out the used paper, allowing it to flap in the wind or to be torn off at regular intervals. The retainer has a take-up spool which captures the used paper neatly.

Serious fishermen often take notes of conditions and results of their efforts on the graph paper as the action takes place. Date, time of day, location can all be jotted down in code on the chart paper, generating a permanent record for duplicating patterns and techniques which proved successful on a particular lake at a given time and circumstance. Retaining the well-documented chart paper can be important when you fish the same area the following year, or even the next day.

Transducer Switch-Over Box

You can purchase a switch box which allows the use of either of two transducers with the same depthfinder. The advantages of this setup are numerous. Perhaps the most important is that it may reduce the need for a second depthfinder. One transducer might be mounted on the transom for use while you're cruising slowly in search of fish and structure. The second transducer could be mounted on the foot of the trolling motor for use when it's time to get serious about a certain spot. The switch box allows a change-over from one transducer to the other any time you choose. In addition to granting multiple use from a single unit, the dual transducer routine can prove valuable in working a narrow creek channel or over a long, slender underwater point. The 10- to 16-foot spread between readings can be a big help when trying to stay on target. The depthfinder can be placed on a swivel mount in the boat so it can be read from any direction. Buying two transducers is a lot cheaper than buying a pair of depthfinders.

Summary

This covers the basics of how sonar works and why it can tell you the distance between your transducer and various underwater objects. By now, the following two pieces of advice should be self-evident. Don't purchase a new sonar unit which has features you will never use, unless they come as standard equipment on the unit which best fits your needs. And, nothing in the world of sonar allows a manufacturer to produce depthfinders at drastically reduced prices, while maintaining quality comparable with more expensive models. You get what you pay for.

Getting Started

3

Installing The Transducer

Many experts say that about half the transducers used today are not installed and/or maintained properly to produce optimum performance. Service repair shops, both factory-operated and independent, say a healthy percentage of complaints from depthfinder owners about their unit's performance can be traced directly back to poor transducer installation. It might be worth noting that the units returned for service obviously came from people who were having severe problems and knew it! There is no way to estimate how many others are having only slightly less-severe problems and don't fully realize what's happening (and not happening) with their unit's performance.

Transducer installation is a bit like tying on the lure before casting into a splashing, feeding school of fish. You know the knot is important, but you get in a big hurry to enjoy the fun which is coming up next. Maybe the average fisherman is so anxious to get on the water that he overlooks the critical importance of proper transducer installation. Maybe he doesn't read the manual carefully (if he even looked at it). In either event, poor installation of a transducer instantly makes it the system's weak link.

The sonar equipment you try so carefully to read on the water cannot produce truly meaningful information if the transducer is poorly installed. It's that basic. The importance of correct procedures in the location and physical installation of your depthfinder transducer cannot be over-emphasized.

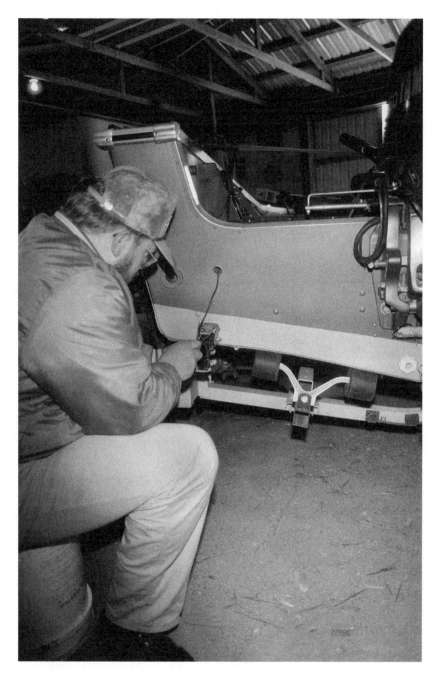

Proper installation of your transducer is keenly important. Be sure to read the installation instructions that come with your unit. The majority of problems that happen on the water stem from a poorly installed transducer.

Installing The Transducer 41

Transducers: What They Can And Cannot Do

Transducers are designed to fire a signal through the water, and then receive that signal after it strikes something and bounces, or reflects, back upward. "Through the water" is the critical part of that description. Transducers cannot shoot (or receive) signals through *air*.

Transducer operation is very simple. You put it under the surface of the water, point it at the bottom, and it works. Fish schools, treetops and various structure have been found on sonar units by simply holding the transducer over the side of the boat. Simple. You can tape the pod to a broom handle or a canoe paddle, stick it beneath the surface and get a good readout on your depthfinder. So why all the fuss?

Aside from getting cramps in your wrist from holding a transducer overboard, you soon discover that boat movement can be a problem. Because most anglers like to use sonar for finding fish while cruising in a moving boat, the transducer must be mounted somehow to maintain proper positioning. In most instances, successful mounting depends upon the speed at which the boat normally will be operating while the depthfinder is in use.

For example, portable depthfinders usually come with the transducer mounted on a metal rod (or a rubber suction cup) which has clamps for attaching it to the boat gunwale. This setup is somewhat similar to taping the puck on a broom handle and lowering it into the water. At very slow boat speeds, the rod and transducer will work just fine in the water. However, as boat speed increases, air bubbles begin to churn around the transducer, resulting in poor readings. And, if the speed is increased further, the rod will bend or pop out of its bracket.

Mounting the transducer on the foot of the electric trolling motor is an excellent choice for slow-motion fish hunting. The trolling motor is used to ease the boat along, and the transducer remains totally submerged. The trolling motor's speed will not cause air bubbles to form on the pod which is usually strapped to the motor housing with oversized radiator hose clamps. The depthfinder and trolling motor electrical systems do not fight each other, so you have a very workable situation with this type of mounting. However, the boat isn't at cruising speed while the depthfinder is in use.

This is where things begin to get tricky. You can mount the

Gunwale And Trolling-Motor Mounting

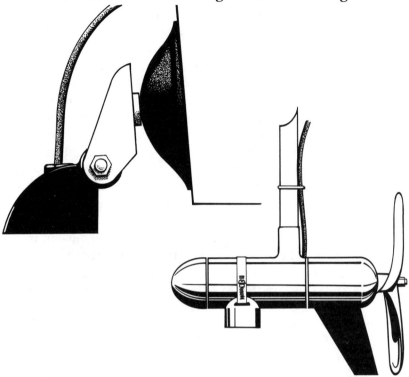

Your transducer must maintain proper positioning after mounting. Some portable depthfinders come with a rubber suction cup for mounting on the gunwale (upper left). Another way of mounting the transducer is on the trolling motor (lower right).

transducer inside the boat, allowing it to shoot signals through the hull, or you can bolt it outside on the bottom of the transom, beneath the water level. Generally speaking, either of the two mountings will allow for medium-to-high-speed readings while the boat is underway. For this reason, most fishermen will opt for one of these procedures. Aluminum boats, however, present a few special considerations for transducer mountings. (This will be explained later in greater detail.)

Through-The-Hull Mounting

Some transducers on the market today are mounted in a hole drilled completely through the hull. A long, threaded shaft on the transducer extends up through the hull where it is secured by washers and a big bolt. Epoxy and waterproof caulking prevent the mount from leaking. The transducer itself stays in the water, snugged up tightly to the underside of the hull. On some boats, especially the larger ones, this mounting works extremely well because big boats rarely go rocketing over stump rows.

Usually, however, through-the-hull mounting means affixing the transducer inside the boat so that the signals are shot through the hull into the water. The advantages of this mounting procedure are numerous. Shooting signals through the hull will eliminate the chance of damage to the transducer if you run over a log, allow for maximum high-speed readings, prevent algae or oil build-up on the eye of the transducer, prevent accidental damage to the transducer from trailering, eliminate the need for holes in the hull or transom and solve a few problems with electrical interference from your big engine.

Many fiberglass-boat builders provide a special cut-out in the rear one-third of the boat, designated as the optimum location for interior mounting of a transducer. Depending upon the expertise of the manufacturer in these matters, the predetermined location is usually the best choice. It may be the only spot on the hull where the transducer can be easily mounted.

The 1978 Flotation Law requires boat manufacturers to install permanently a certain amount of foam flotation materials into most boats under 20 feet in length. Frequently, this foam is placed next to the hull beneath the flooring, and normally is needed most in exactly the spot where you wish to put the transducer. Transducers cannot shoot a signal through foam.

Similarly, product liability insurance costs have caused many manufacturers to improve the structural integrity of their boat hulls. This has resulted in plywood strips being glassed into the hull in the rear one-third of the boat, the use of false floors with air space between the hull and deck and the use of a balsa wood layer joined to the hull over all, or part, of the inner surface. As you might expect, transducers cannot shoot signals through any of these materials.

Faced with a fiberglass boat lacking a factory cut-out for mounting the transducer, and finding that one of the above construction techniques was used for added strength in the hull, you have a decision to make. You can cut, drill and cuss your way through the foam and flooring until you reach the thin glass shell, or you can hang the transducer off the transom. If you decide to

Through-The-Hull Mounting

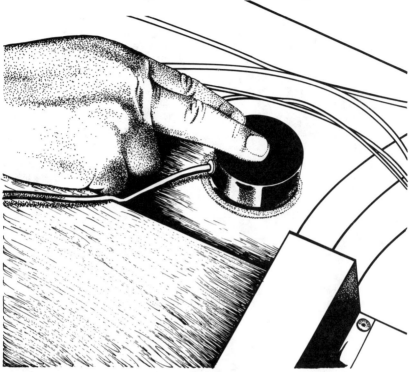

Through-the-hull mounting allows the transducer signals to be shot through the boat's hull into the water. Epoxy prevents the mount from leaking. There are many advantages to this mounting procedure; however, it can be frustrating doing it yourself.

make your own mounting spot, you must be sure to reach exactly the raw fiberglass hull. Going too far with the blade will puncture the hull; stopping short of the raw glass leaves signal-deadening material between your transducer and the optimum readings you want to receive.

If you really want to mount your transducer inside the boat, you should hire the factory people to do it. (This is an extremely good idea because, at this point, you aren't exactly sure where the optimum location is, anyway. And, once the deed is done, it's too late to change your mind!)

Fortunately, not all glass boats have this layer of foam and/or wood in the back end. If your boat has the factory-determined, cut-out location, mount the transducer there and hope they had it figured out correctly. If there is no set spot designated and you find

Plywood strips are often used for reinforcement strength in many fiberglass boat hulls. If you're mounting the transducer inside the hull, you'll need to cut through these strips in order for it to work effectively.

Complete Angler's Library

an area where the raw hull is accessible, you'll still have to do a bit of experimenting before selecting the final resting place for your transducer.

Clean out the sump area diligently with warm, soapy water. Drain the water; rinse out the area well. Refill the sump with fresh water to a depth of perhaps 2 inches. Go to the lake and have someone drive the boat for you *carefully* while you peer over the transom. (The boat should be running at half-throttle or slightly better.) Watch for a spot on the transom where there is the least amount of turbulence coming from underneath the moving boat. Mark that spot.

Next, anchor the boat over a drop-off or some underwater trees in about 30 feet of water. The structure can be found easily by holding the transducer in your hand while searching and coasting. When the boat is still, turn the depthfinder on full power (i.e., crank the sensitivity knob wide open.) You are now ready to choose the optimum spot in the sump for mounting your transducer. The water in the sump will provide good contact between the transducer and the hull. Rub away any air bubbles which may form on the two surfaces. With the depthfinder still running, move the puck around on the hull in the immediate vicinity of the mark on the transom. When you find a spot which appears to give the best depthfinder readings on the face of your depthfinder, mark it with an "X" on the hull. Now, you must do more testing.

Holding the transducer in your hand, put it over the side and completely beneath the water's surface. Compare the detail now showing on your depthfinder from the hand-held pod with the detail you observed when shooting signals through the hull. Because the boat is stationary, you should be looking at the identical structure below. A major difference in the two readings can only mean that you have a subfloor, foam or something else beneath the sump. Yes, that means you have a problem. Continue the experiments to find a location in the sump which provides comparable detail with the hand-held readings. If you can't find one, you must either cut through the subfloor or mount the transducer on the transom.

On the brighter side, if you find only minor differences between the two readings, you're in business. Go home and finish the job.

Drain and dry the bilge (sump) area. Sand the selected mounting location down to the raw fiberglass with sandpaper. Remove dust and debris from that spot when you finish. Be sure no paint chips or other foreign matter remain in the circle you made with the sander.

Some manufacturers recommend building a small dam or enclosure around the mounting circle. This helps prevent the securing agent—usually epoxy cement—from running. It's a good idea. Making sure the boat (trailer) is level also helps.

Experts recommend using a two-part epoxy cement for securing the transducer to the hull. Silicone is not recommended as it will remain a gel beneath the pod for quite some time, reducing the sensitivity of readings. Oil and gas spills also affect silicone, eventually ruining the installation.

Select a two-part epoxy with a fairly long drying time. The 30-minute variety is better than the five-minute variety because the fast-curing epoxy has a tendency to generate heat while it cures. Heat can cause the creation of air bubbles, a definite "no-no" for optimum transducer performance.

Mix the epoxy slowly and carefully in a container. Do not enthusiastically whip the mixture because that will cause air bubbles. Place a coating of epoxy on the face of the transducer and set it aside. Pour the remaining cement onto the hull within the mounting circle. Although not necessary, a hair dryer can be used for a few seconds to heat the epoxy. This thins the mixture slightly, reducing the chance of air bubbles.

Place the transducer face into position on the hull, pushing down firmly and working it gently to force out air and excess cement. Air must not be left beneath the puck! Once the transducer is in position on the hull, place a weight on top of it and let the cement dry for several hours. Stay out of the boat while it's drying.

Transom Mounting
Procedures and "angle of attack" vary from one manufacturer to the next. However, the instruction manual that comes with your depthfinder generally does a good job explaining the proper installation method for transom mounting. Here are some tips that do not appear in most instruction manuals. Mounting the transducer on the boat transom is the easiest and fastest installation method, and it allows accurate readings at cruising speeds. It's a mounting system which is easily changed, and lets you swap

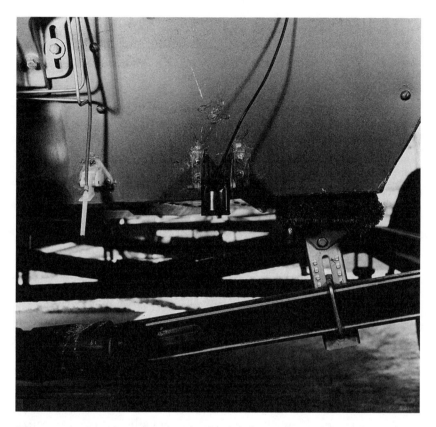

This transom-mounted transducer was placed with the boat trailer in mind. You don't want the transducer interfering with trailering; it's very hard on transducers.

transducers any time you choose. However, it increases the chance of damage to the transducer. This is because the transducer can be struck by foreign objects, and its position requires closer attention to water turbulence caused by slight irregularities in installation. It also demands more attention to maintenance of the transducer than interior mounting does.

Mounting procedure begins with the same "looking over the transom while running" procedure as for hull mounting. When making this check, mark two places on the transom which show the smoothest water so you can examine the choice spots later when the boat is sitting on the trailer.

You should mark a pair of smooth-water locations on the transom for two reasons: When the boat is on the trailer, it is easier to see if placing a transducer in either location will interfere with the act of trailering the boat or if it will be touched by the bunks or carpeted runners on the trailer itself. In the case of an aluminum boat, you can decide which spot has the least number of rivets and hull irregularities in front of it by examining the next 6 to 8 feet of hull toward the bow. It is possible that the hull irregularities you discovered were not creating excessive turbulence because of the speed the boat was traveling when you made your observation. A faster or slower speed could make a big difference.

Choose the location which is not affected by trailering the boat, and which would be least affected by hull irregularities forward of that particular spot. Because the transom mount positions the transducer under the hull and water, you can bypass the exercise of comparing readings between hand-held signals and potential location signals. Once the decision has been made on the best spot for installation, take a deep breath and start drilling holes in your boat.

Most problems with transom mounts come from either the lack of a smooth joining between transducer and hull, or an improper angle on the transducer face. Some try to put the face of the transducer exactly flush with the bottom of the boat, but they leave a gap between the transom and the transducer. This gap simply creates turbulence that wasn't there before. A carefully smoothed-over "bridge" of silicone between the two surfaces can eliminate the problem. However, don't get silicone on the face of the transducer.

Some transom-mounted transducers work better if they are dropped well below the hull level. Then, the transducer can cut its own way through the water without regard to what is happening a half-inch above its smooth, pointed nose. The risk of hitting a submerged object is greatly increased, but, usually, so is its performance.

The "angle of attack" means only the amount of tilt you give the face of the transducer in the water. The recommended angle is provided in the instructions, although most anglers cannot estimate a 6-degree angle. Here again, experiment a bit on the water until you find the best position, then use lock washers and a little muscle to keep the transducer in that position.

For those who don't like to get wet, use a liberal amount of silicone sealer in and around the holes you drilled in the transom for the mounting bracket(s). You will find that neatly and accu-

Transom Mounting

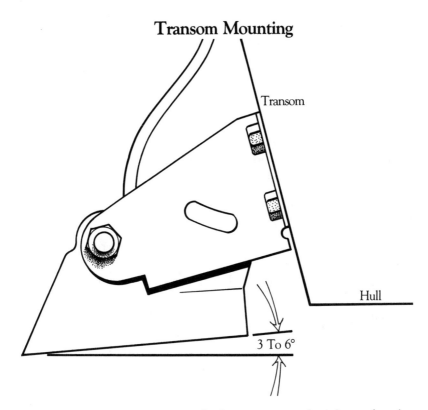

Some problems with transom mounts are related to an improper angle on the transducer face. The angle of attack is the amount of tilt the transducer face has in the water. A 3- to 6-degree angle is recommended, but experiment until you find the best position.

rately marking the holes for the bracket will help prevent all sorts of problems.

Finally, bumping during trailering and water pressure while the boat is running can eventually change the "angle of attack" on the transom-mounted transducer if the bolts and washers securing them are not tight. A tilt change can cause the puck to perform poorly. As a precaution, you should check the tilt often during the season.

Finishing The Job Properly

With the transducer properly secured, either inside the boat or on the transom, the task remains of installing the depthfinder itself. It must be mounted, and the wires for the electrical system routed away from possible interference. The unit can be bolted down almost anywhere you wish; however, there are a few points to consider.

When you've chosen a spot, check for clearance all around the depthfinder. You don't want the back of the unit jammed against a windshield where the cords will be kinked or rubbed bare with vibration, or where the plug-ins for power and transducer cords must be bent to the side under pressure. Nor do you want the face of the unit perched within inches of the steering wheel so you can't adjust the knobs while steering the boat. In the case of a graph, clearance is needed in front of the unit so you can change rolls of paper, or make notes, without removing the unit from its mount. With it pushed up against the steering wheel, you can't open the cover on the graph's face.

Be sure you have good clearance on all sides of your depth-finder before drilling holes in the console for the mounting bracket. Also, check to see what happens when you turn on the unit when it's near a magnetic compass. Frequently, the two do not make good neighbors; they constantly bicker about priority.

Finally, sit in the boat's driver's seat to see if the unit face will be clearly visible in its chosen spot. Unfortunately, many boat consoles are sloped at an angle which makes mounting depth' finders a difficult task.

Also, you should consider the benefits of twisting the bracket slightly toward the passenger side of the boat before making it a permanent fixture. (This is so your partner can watch the events below, too.)

The mechanics of mounting the depthfinder bracket are simple enough. Mark the location for the holes neatly and accurately. Drill the holes so you can use large bolts for securing the bracket to your console. (This is quite important to the life of your depth-finder.) Boat vibrations from pounding waves or even a small chop on the water will eventually loosen the bracket if it is not heavily secured. When allowed to rattle and shake, the depth-finder will need a trip to the repairman too soon. Expensive and sophisticated circuitry was never designed to survive the rigors of life in a paint mixer.

Once the location for your unit has been carefully considered and the mounting bracket securely attached to your boat, you face still another problem. The power and transducer cords which plug into your unit can be extremely finicky. Sometimes, they will per-

Sometimes, you will have to improvise. The surface angles on some boat consoles are not designed to handle mounted depthfinders. In this case, a 2x8 board was used as the mount's base.

form admirably in close proximity to other wiring within the boat, while sometimes they seem to pick up the smallest amount of static from other sources.

Static, or electrical interference, can make your days on the water seem like a week without a Friday. Every time you think you have figured out how to read the signals on your sonar equipment, you will observe miscellaneous images on your flasher or graph which defy interpretation. You must eliminate the problem. And, the best time to eliminate the problem from electrical interference is before it happens.

It is important that you wire the depthfinder directly to your main battery instead of plugging the power cord into a spare jack beneath the console. Some sonar manufacturers agree with this; some don't. Going straight to the main battery avoids possible noise pick-up from other equipment in the boat. The experts all agree on that. At least one sonar expert says if you wire the depth-finder through the dashboard, it can make a change in the nega-tive lead which goes to that dashboard. This causes electrolysis which, in time, will eat up the transducer.

Other problems resulting from a dashboard hookup include a slight loss of power in the connection, or in the size wire used by the boat builder, and a power loss resulting from running various accessories in the boat simultaneously with the depthfinder. Why gamble? Most depthfinders come equipped with sufficient lengths of power cord to reach from mid-ship to the battery compartment. Spend another 79 cents for tape to keep the wire out of your way along its route from the unit to the battery.

You also face the challenge of calculating the route of the depthfinder power cord and the wire from the transducer so that neither of them gets chummy with other electrical wires in your boat. This can be frustrating, especially when the wiring for so many modern bass boats looks like an octopus hatchery. Organize that mess to the best of your ability, and tape the wires for your depthfinder out of the way. Creativity has certain rewards. The little plastic ties you buy at the hardware store are great for this.

Run the transducer cord along a path which will keep it the maximum distance away from all other wires in the boat, espe-cially those in the electrical system of your big engine and its ta-chometer. Flexible metal conduit, plastic hose pipe and liberal layers of electrical tape wrapped around the cord will all help shield the transducer cord from unwanted interference.

You should also install a small fuse breaker on the positive wire going from the depthfinder to your battery. (You can purchase these pieces of insurance from practically any automotive parts dealer.) Splice them into the wire, and rest easy on the water while the sonar unit is in operation. The owner's manual for the depthfinder should state the appropriate size fuse to use; however, if it omits this data, try a four-amp fuse for safety. The fuse should be inserted into the positive lead approximately 12 inches from the battery. Overheated wires can cause fires, and fuses are cheap compared to replacing a whole boat!

There is more to installing a depthfinder system in your boat than most people think. If the installation of your transducer or the unit wiring is done poorly, you will have lost a great deal of efficiency before ever getting on the water.

Aluminum Hulls: Unanswered Controversy

The advances in sonar technology have been fantastic. However, there is one question that has not been fully answered: Can a signal from a transducer be shot through an aluminum boat hull effectively?

Sides were clearly drawn on the issue in the early 1980s. Brand X manufacturer stated a very positive "yes," while Brand Y said "no" with equal conviction. Nobody had done enough controlled testing to make a positive statement of fact. Given the growing popularity of aluminum fishing boats at the time, "through the hull" abilities of transducers in aluminum boats was an important consideration. Obviously, it still is today.

Aluminum boats have special characteristics which definitely affect the performance of a depthfinder transducer, whether mounted inside or on the transom.

When considering inside, or through-the-hull mounting, remember that different manufacturers construct their hulls in a variety of thickness. Some hulls are coated with a layer or two of paint, while others are "raw" metal. Then, too, there are differences in alloy content between types of aluminum. Construction techniques make some aluminum boats quite rigid; others are rather flexible. This means some metal boats vibrate a lot while running; some do not. All of these factors affect the transducer's efficiency.

Whether mounting your transducer inside the boat or hanging it off the transom, remember that aluminum boats are "built" a piece at a time, not poured or sprayed into a mold for single-piece construction. Pieces are cut, and then assembled with rivets and/or welds. Those welded spots and rivet heads, plus any keels, steps, runners or scoops for the livewell plug, create water turbulence as the boat moves across the lake. That turbulence takes the form of air bubbles which flow under the hull and exit beneath the transom. And, remember, transducers cannot effectively shoot a signal through air—or air bubbles.

Life is more complicated for the aluminum boat sonar user if you think about the manner in which many of these craft bounce their flat little bottoms over the water. The moment the engine raises the flat-bottomed fishing machine onto a plane (even on

Aluminum boats are built one piece at a time. The resulting welds and rivet heads can create water turbulence ahead of the transducer, causing many problems. You should experiment with different mounting methods before permanent installation.

very smooth water), air is trapped beneath the hull. No matter what type of water you're on, it happens this way: The bow goes up, air hits the flat undersurface, and the air gets trapped momentarily while it passes under the hull. A light chop on the water produces an excessive amount of air traveling beneath the hull.

Weight distribution in the boat can be used to combat these problems. The more batteries, gas cans and concrete blocks you stack in the general vicinity of the transducer, the deeper that particular portion of the boat will ride. The more weight you place forward, the lower the bow will ride when on a plane.

Mounting your transducer on the transom, and dropping it down well below the level of your hull, is one answer. One large manufacturer markets a bracket today designed to do exactly that. Presumably, the transducer then could care less about all the fuss just above its head.

Many anglers still are unable to get good readings when shooting transducer signals through an aluminum hull. In some cases, it seems the entire hull becomes something of a sounding board for the pulses, and the returning information gets a bit fuzzy. Other boats with lighter-gauge metal, different alloy content or less "flex" in the bottom may allow through-the-hull transducer operation without significant loss of detail. You will need to experiment with your boat before making a decision.

Hanging the transducer off the transom and building a smooth bridge of silicone across the gap will solve the problem. Select the location for mounting in the manner previously described for finding "smooth water" exiting beneath the transom. If your day on the water includes trying to read your depthfinder while zipping over the lake at 65 mph, this type of mount will not provide optimum readout in the process. But, if you're using sonar primarily for the purpose of searching for fish and structure at reduced boat speeds, this method of mounting a transducer on an aluminum boat will work admirably.

By all means, experiment with the mounting method in your aluminum boat. It is quite possible you will be able to find a spot inside the boat where you can shoot a signal effectively from your transducer. It is also equally possible you will lose far too much detail to use through-the-hull mounting. Compare signals shot through the metal with signals generated while hand-holding the transducer over the side. You, then, be the judge.

All who fish from aluminum boats should be aware of problems connected with either mounting a transducer in the hull or merely hanging one over the transom. There is nothing wrong with your choice of boats; you just have to adapt your sonar mounting procedure to overcome the obstacles.

One major depthfinder manufacturer suggests the following procedure for mounting a transducer to shoot signals through an aluminum hull:

1. Select a clean, flat surface area between the grooves or rivets in the hull, and sand the area smoothly to insure good contact.

2. Mix two-part epoxy cement thoroughly for several minutes, then apply a liberal amount of the cement onto the face of the transducer, spreading evenly.

3. Any remaining epoxy should be applied to the inside hull location for the transducer.

4. Position the transducer in the site, using a circular motion to squeeze out all air bubbles.

5. Press down firmly and hold the transducer in place for a few minutes to complete the job.

Properly affixed, the transducer should perform at all speeds.

Your first step in mounting a transducer through an aluminum hull is to select a clean, flat surface between the hull's grooves or rivets. Then, sand that area, making it as smooth as possible. This will help insure good contact.

A Second Depthfinder Up Front

Having two depthfinders in the boat definitely makes life easier for the fisherman. You can cruise the lake searching for a likely spot with a console-mounted unit, traveling at whatever speed you choose. Once fish are found, the big engine is killed, and so is the console depthfinder. The bow-mounted second unit then takes over as it allows you to center the boat over your quarry and hold it there with a little help from the trolling motor.

Placement of the front transducer is optional. A few fiberglass boats are designed with front cut-outs in the hull for mounting the forward transducer. This will work fine when the boat is resting, but not while running on plane. When the boat is up and going, the bow normally is lifted out of the water by the steps, lifters and strakes built into the hull. And, this would, of course, put air between the hull and the water up front.

Another choice of location for the second transducer would be back on the transom again. This is not a particularly good place for it, because the signals you would be reading from the bow-mounted unit would be some 10 to 15 feet away from your tennis shoes, instead of directly below them. Fish you see on your depthfinder would be fish living beneath your transom, not under the bow. Vertical jigging for fish 15 feet away from your lure is not often very productive.

The ideal place for mounting your front-unit transducer is on the foot of your trolling motor. You can't run the boat's big engine while the trolling motor is in the water, but it really doesn't matter because the unit mounted on the console will be used while cruising anyway. With the pod mounted on the trolling motor, fish you see will be fish under your feet.

There are three easy ways to mount a transducer on your trolling motor. The simplest is applying a glob of silicone to the top of the puck, and squashing it onto the bottom of the motor housing. String or rubber bands will hold the puck in place while the silicone dries. Route the cord well clear of the prop and on up the shaft, using plastic ties. Silicone is fine for this because there should be no oil spills in this area.

Some manufacturers supply an oversized radiator hose clamp, and build "ears" on their transducer for use in mounting it to the trolling motor. Insert the clamp through the holes in the ears, take it on around the motor housing and then tighten the screw to hold everything in place—simple and efficient. Route the cord in the same manner as above.

A third method for mounting the puck on the electric motor is rather unconventional, but it works quite well. It also can solve problems in mounting when the transducer's top surface is not designed to fit solidly against the bottom of the housing. Find a rubber suction cup that is supplied with a portable depthfinder's transducer. Other types of suction cups will work, too, provided they are large enough and can be attached to a bracket.

The suction cup is mated with a transducer bracket, and the puck installed in the bracket. The suction cup is then pushed against the bottom of the motor housing, held securely with a pair of plastic ties. This way, you can mount a transducer which was not designed to fit flush with the bottom of a trolling motor, and it will perform admirably. In addition, the short stem on the rubber cup will flex slightly, cushioning the transducer against any contact with stumps and rocks in shallow water.

Bow-mounted depthfinders are usually placed in the boat a bit forward of the front seat where the angler in that seat can read it easily. It is recommended that you wire the unit directly to your

When a boat speeds and gets up on plane, the bow rises out of the water. Therefore, transducers used for reading while at cruising speeds must be mounted in the rear third of the boat.

boat's main battery. If the power cord doesn't reach from bow to battery, it can be extended the needed inches (or feet) with automotive wire (No. 12 or No. 14). If you wish to solder the connection between the two wires, use a rosin-core solder, not one with an acid core.

Concluding Comments

Before closing out this chapter on transducers, it should be mentioned that, with a few boats, the simplest method for installing your transducer is not to install it at all! If your boat has an enclosed sump area, and the hull directly beneath it is of single-layer construction, this may work for you.

Pour about an inch of water into the sump, place your transducer in with it and go fishing. The water in the sump will keep the puck's face well-wetted, so it will shoot signals right through the hull perfectly. You don't have to cement the puck to the floor, just toss it in there and be sure the water covers it.

There are a couple of problems with this procedure. You must keep the sump area clean and free of oil or gas. If you drop a bar of Ivory soap into the water along with the transducer, the soap will help prevent oil from coating the eye. It would be wise to clean out the sump area often, for the same reason. And if you hit rough water, which makes the transducer bounce around a bit, you may have to reach back there afterward and stand it upright again. Still, this is certainly the easiest way to "mount" a transducer if your boat design will allow it.

Remember that your transducer's eye can become totally blinded if it comes into contact with oil for any period of time. Oil soaks into the transducer's face, first reducing its sensitivity a good deal, then finally coating the surface sufficiently to ruin its operation completely. Transom-mounted transducers are subject to contact oil while the boat is just sitting in a busy marina. Road film accumulated in transit to and from the lake can build up on a transducer, also. It is important to keep the face of the transducer clean. Wash it often with warm water and soap. Obviously, this does not apply to transducers cemented into the hull inside the boat, but you should check on them occasionally, too. Be sure no cracks in the cement have developed which could allow oil or gas to seep under the pod.

=========4=========

Operating Your Depthfinder

P roperly installed and functioning, a depthfinder will produce a wealth of valuable information for any fisherman.
The amount of information you get is limited only by
the circuitry purchased and your ability to read and interpret the signals.

It is a simple fact that expertise in reading a sonar unit does
not come quickly. It doesn't even come slowly. Sometimes, it
comes *very* slowly. Some of the advertisements for sonar units
make it all sound so easy, but out there in the lake where fish are
to be found, it just doesn't work that way. Learning to understand
all the information your depthfinder is providing requires a great
many hours of serious work, study and experimentation. Most of
which should take place on the water.

This chapter contains a lot of information on how to operate
your sonar equipment correctly. There may be information here
that was not included in your unit's instruction manual. Hope-
fully, it will save you many long hours trying to figure it out by trial
and error.

The information presented here is based upon the assumption
that you have properly installed your transducer and have made
the correct electrical connections for the unit.

Controlling Sensitivity

An expert on depthfinders once said that the most common
mistake people make with their depthfinder takes place when they

When you have your depthfinder fine-tuned, you'll be able to zero-in on fish like this nice bass. And, as you'll discover in this book, you can tell if they're willing to bite or not.

Operating Your Depthfinder   63

The angler's most common mistake is failing to turn the sensitivity control up sufficiently. The more you "turn the volume up," the higher the sensitivity level.

turn the switch on! And, it's true. This observation is backed by several other sonar experts, and even hinted at in a few manufacturers' owner's manuals.

The "Off/On" switch for a depthfinder is the power control, acting much like the volume knob on a radio. It also performs the job of "fine tuning" the frequency just as the other knob on a radio is used to zero-in on a station for the best reception. The gain, or sensitivity control as it is often called, simply activates the unit and then increases the power to the receiver depending on how far the knob is turned. The more you "turn the volume up," the more power you have, and the more sensitivity you get.

Most anglers turn on their depthfinder, continue rotating the sensitivity knob until they get a bottom reading, and then stop right there. "Stopping right there" is the mistake.

If you continue to increase the power, you will get a second reading, or "echo," at exactly twice the actual bottom depth. This is caused by part of the initial signal coming back to the top of the lake after striking the bottom, bouncing off the water surface itself (and/or the hull of your boat) and being reflected back down to the bottom where it strikes again and is bounced upward for the second time. Because of the elapsed time while making two round trips, the "second" echo will be recorded on your unit at twice the actual depth of the bottom. If it were not for the fact that high-frequency sonar signals are partially absorbed by the objects they strike, the routine could go on forever.

When you pass over a very hard bottom (like an old roadbed, for example), you immediately can see an increase in multiple bottom readings, each appearing on the unit in increments of the actual depth. Hard surfaces reflect more of the signal than soft surfaces (an important fact to remember).

Having more than one bottom reading on the depthfinder annoys many people, so they turn down the sensitivity until only one can be seen. Reducing the unit's power, however, may rob it of the needed sensitivity to pick up and display the smaller, weaker underwater echoes. You know, like the ones that come from fish ...

Other benefits are derived from having a second bottom reading shown on your depthfinder, in addition to furnishing sufficient power for displaying weaker signals. These will be explained shortly. But, for now, remember that giving your depthfinder enough power and sensitivity to create a second bottom echo will also give it enough muscle to display fish.

As the power is increased, the initial bottom reading widens on both flashers and graphs. This in no way affects what the unit is telling you about the correct water depth. The band, or bottom signal, will widen in a downward direction only. The top of that reading remains constant, showing the accurate distance between your transducer and the lake's bottom. The bottom reading band expands because part of your signal is being absorbed by the bottom itself, thus slightly delaying the return echo. That moving wheel or belt on your unit turns too fast to be seen by the human eye. Thus, it's only reasonable that even a fractional difference in the time lapse for a returning signal would be shown farther down the scale.

There are times when a second bottom echo is not desirable. When you are fishing with a flasher unit and the bottom depth exceeds half the maximum depth on the face of your unit, the second reading would appear somewhere in the area on the dial where you hope to see fish signals. For example, on a flasher with a 60-foot depth scale, a second echo for the bottom in 40 feet of water would show up at 20 feet on the face of the unit. (40 + 40 − 60 = 20). This may be the exact depth you hope to find huge stripers, and it would be tough to separate their signals from those created by the second bottom echo. In this case, turn the sensitivity control down only until the second reading fades. The stripers will generate bright signals at 20 feet, not weak ones.

Depth Scales

Many sonar units have two or more depth scales from which to choose. A flip of the switch or a pull on the knob will convert the overall depth scale from one set of numbers to another. Advantages here are numerous. As mentioned, when water depth exceeds half the maximum reading on your flasher, the second echo from the bottom can cover fish signals in the productive zone. If you have the multiple-scale feature on your unit, you can switch over to a deeper scale and eliminate the problem. On graph units, when the water depth exceeds the total depth shown on a particular scale, the bottom reading simply disappears. In this case, you switch to a deeper scale to find the bottom again.

It is important that you adjust the sensitivity control to handle the deeper scale settings. Usually, changing over to a deeper depth scale on a sonar unit requires an increase in power to maintain maximum readout efficiency.

Under some conditions, it can be advantageous to switch to a very shallow depth scale on graphs. This allows the unit to display detail over the entire width of the paper. With enlarged detail, it is much easier to identify fish and types of structure. Sometimes, in order to track suspended fish, you may want to sacrifice your bottom reading. It depends upon the situation.

Most graphs, liquid crystal and video units are programmed to allow the selection of a specific band, or layer, of water, and then expand the detail "full-size" on the paper or screen. You merely enter the upper and lower limits of the desired depth, and the machine does the rest. Your choice may be flexible, as with a moving

This LCR unit has four depth ranges (0-15, 0-30, 0-60 and 0-120 feet) that can be controlled automatically by its microcomputer, or manually with the range control button. Here, it is set at 30 feet, revealing the bottom reading at 27. (Notice the fish located at approximately 6 feet.)

cursor on video, or broken into predetermined increments.

As a general rule, you should use the most shallow depth scale on both flashers and graphs which allows the unit to cover the total water depth. This makes it much easier to read the signals (and, is far less confusing). However, when the bottom drops materially, switch over to a deeper depth scale and turn up the sensitivity a bit.

Suppressor Knob

This particular adjustment on your sonar unit should be eyed with caution, like a shabbily dressed bill collector. The suppressor is designed to filter out unwanted interference in your unit, much like the squelch control in a CB radio. Sometimes, like over-eager salesmen, it doesn't know when to stop performing. Although use of the suppressor control generally does not affect the unit's sensitivity, it has an adverse effect on the way some of the smaller underwater objects are displayed.

The suppressor causes a "blending" phenomenon. Small objects close together in the water frequently are displayed on the face of your equipment as a single image. Fish relaxing close to the bottom can be merged into the bottom signals and never be seen. Three or four small fish getting friendly in a small area could be shown as a single trophy worthy of attention.

Unwanted noise from your electrical system, or the engine's ignition can cause false signals to appear on your depthfinder. Air bubbles on the transducer can do the same thing. Cavitation in a spinning prop can screw up readings, also. These "noise" problems are why your unit has a suppressor control. Limited adjustment of the suppressor will normally make them go away. Just remember that the less suppression control used, the better the differentiation between individual objects below. At slow boat speeds, no suppression should be needed.

While on the subject of a depthfinder's suppression control, it seems only appropriate to talk about the cause and elimination of unwanted signal "static" which can appear on the depthfinder. The suppressor circuitry should be used only as a "last ditch" effort to clarify readings. Problems causing static interference usually can be eliminated before use of this feature is needed. If you experience numerous unwanted static signals on your depthfinder, even while running at slow speeds, try the following procedure to eliminate the source(s):

Turn off the big engine and allow the boat to come to a complete stop in the water. All static signals should then disappear. If not, check to see if there is any other electrical equipment running in the boat. If the problem is coming from some accessory you are running, you must rewire the gadget if you wish to use it simultaneously with the depthfinder.

If all static interference disappears when the boat stops moving and the engine is killed, your problem is caused by either engine ignition interference or air bubbles on the transducer. To find out which is the culprit, put the engine in neutral and rev it up. If the static comes back, you know the engine's electrical system is at fault. You will need to re-route the wires going to your depthfinder, keeping them farther away from all electrical wires to the big engine. You may be forced to encase the transducer cord in a plastic hose, wrap it several times with electrical tape, or maybe choose a different type of spark plug for your engine. Contact the engine manufacturer for suggestions about how to reduce ignition interference.

If those remedies fail, you are getting excess air turbulence on the face of your transom-mounted transducer, or you are getting cavitation noises from the prop. Adjust the transducer angle of attack. Check to see if any silicone bridge between hull and transducer has broken or wrinkled. Slide the puck farther down into the water on its bracket. If that doesn't work, find another location for mounting your transducer, preferably farther away from the prop.

Other Important Features

Most graphs have an additional pair of controls not found on flashers. Both are rather dramatic in the results they can produce. The chart speed control determines the speed at which paper is fed through the graph. The grayline or whiteline control shades the bottom reading for easier identification of objects near the bottom.

Most anglers are cautious with money, and, therefore, tend to be stingy on the subject of chart speed. Anglers often fail to see the advantage of running paper through their graph at maximum speed. Yet, there are many times when a fast chart speed is necessary for getting meaningful readout on the paper.

The most easily-understood example will occur when you motor across a small creek bed looking for fish and productive structure. With the paper speed set at a slow pace, details of the creek bed, and everything in it, will appear compressed tightly together. You may see little more than a "crack" in the bottom. This is because you passed over the creek bed and exited across the far shoulder before the graph paper had time to draw out the details for you.

Conversely, the use of a higher paper speed would have allowed the graph to expand, or spread out the detail as you went over the area. Instead of seeing only a thin crack in the earth below, you would be able to observe the drop-off on both sides of the creek, channel structure and, probably, fish relaxing nearby. So here you see the advantage in using a fast paper speed on your

Chart Paper Speed

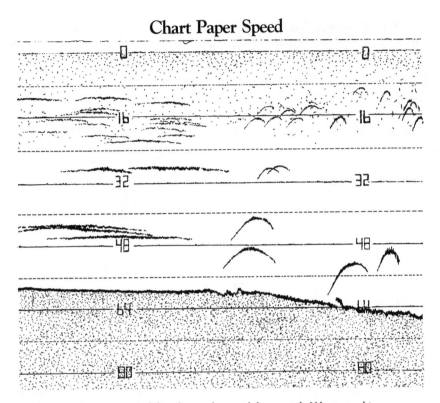

Setting your chart paper speed directly correlates with boat speed. If boat speed increases, so should chart speed. If boat speed decreases, so should chart speed. A very slow boat speed combined with a fast paper speed will distort the graph's typical arched figures (at right) which represent fish, causing them to appear as near straight horizontal lines (at left).

graph: You get more detail and you see it more clearly, at least most of the time. In principle, the same generally goes for video sweep speed.

When talking about chart paper speed for getting better detail, the discussion must include the subject of boat speed. As a general rule, the faster the boat is moving, the faster the chart speed must be to keep up. It follows that the slower the boat moves, the slower you can run the paper through the machine without suffering a great loss of detail. Beyond those generalities, you will be forced to experiment with your own setup, trying different combinations of boat/paper speeds until you find the system which compresses the least detail for you on carbon-backed pine trees or micro imagery.

A very slow paper speed will distort the typical arched figure drawn by the graph as you pass over fish, causing them to appear as near-straight vertical lines. An excessively slow boat speed will stretch out fish signals because the critter remains beneath the transducer for longer time periods. In this case, instead of getting the arched image on the graph, you observe a long, almost straight horizontal line. An extreme example of this would be where the boat, transducer and fish were all sitting still. Only the graph paper is moving. You would see the bottom reading and the straight line representing the depth of the fish which will just keep going on, and on and on.

You will have to run many rolls of graph paper through your machine before mastering the proper relation between boat speed and chart paper speed under various conditions.

The grayline or whiteline control on many graphs also can be difficult to use effectively. Its function is to shade away the heavy black mass drawn on the paper directly below where the bottom reading is shown, leaving in its place a single black line representing the correct bottom depth. This exercise in electronic genius makes it far easier to distinguish trees and brush on the bottom, and makes it even easier to spot fish holding near the bottom.

Another advantage to having the grayline feature is that it helps you determine the bottom composition. Hard bottoms cause the gray area to widen on the graph. When the bottom changes to mud or vegetation, the signals are weaker causing the gray area to shrink automatically.

Excess use of the grayline control will cause unwanted shading of all large objects in the water. Big fish, schools of smaller fish, treetops and other things in the water will be shaded just like the bottom, making it more difficult to accurately figure out what you are seeing on the paper.

Miscellaneous Points About Operation

Very high boat speed will compress the detail on your graph, regardless of the paper speed. High boat speed will make the "blips" on a flasher almost impossible to read, too. You can observe bottom depth fairly accurately on a depthfinder while the boat is steaming along (provided you have a good transducer installation), but reading detail accurately on either a flasher or graph when the boat is traveling in excess of 30 mph will be virtually impossible.

When the transducer is moving at high boat speeds, detail on the graph will be highly compressed. However, you can identify bottom depth with a depthfinder that has a properly installed transducer.

Complete Angler's Library

With some graphs, turning the sensitivity control wide open will cause excessive black printing (or burning, to be more accurate) on the paper. The detail will have a tendency to smear, and the carbon buildup gets pretty bad. These units are designed to be turned up only until you get a good second bottom reading. Their ability to provide power beyond this point is reserved for deeper water situations. The smearing effect makes it tough to read the images accurately, and the excess dust created while burning the paper makes it necessary to clean away the particles inside the case frequently.

Do not increase the white/grayline control knob sufficiently to shade the second bottom echo. Only the first bottom reading should be shaded. This has nothing to do with the amount of sensitivity you give to the unit.

Optimum readout on a paper graph comes from matching boat speed to paper speed in the unit. The goal is to spread out the detail on the paper so that images are easily identified. The faster the boat passes over the bottom, the more detail the graph will display on any given stretch of paper. (The detail becomes more compressed as boat speed increases.) The opposite is true when the boat is merely drifting in the wind. You should experiment with combinations of boat and paper speed until you are satisfied with how the readout appears. Generally, the best results come with the paper speed set at three-fourths full while the boat motors along at just above idle speed.

Increasing sensitivity on any depthfinder, flasher or graph will improve the unit's ability to display fish signals from the outer edge of the transducer cone.

Slower paper speeds generate slightly darker images on graph paper. Excess sensitivity control usage results in very dark images drawn on the graph paper, sometimes making them hard to read and interpret. Concentrations of plankton and baitfish in the water are likely to be shown as a single huge mass, giving rise to fears that "Jaws" is prowling around in your lake.

At one time, you could not simultaneously operate two depthfinders of similar frequency in your boat. This was because the units would pick up signals from each other, causing a "cartwheel" effect on flashers, and pure jumble on a graph. Most machines on the market today have a filtering procedure which separates the signals. However, unless both units in your boat have this feature, one of them is going to be affected anyway. The same holds true for depthfinders operating in other boats nearby.

The fish you see on your depthfinder probably are not as close together as they appear. This is due to the mechanical transition which occurs by taking everything within a circle of viewing area and placing it onto a flat plane. The transducer cone of signals covers several feet on the bottom, and the fish you see displayed can be anywhere within that area. They are not stacked on top of each other down there.

The deeper in the water fish signals appear, the more likely the fish itself is off to one side or the other from your boat. This is due to the spread of the cone as it goes down, and the "law of averages," which says only a small part of the fish in a given circle will be directly under your transducer at any particular time. In the case of a graph unit, you can see when the fish is closest to your transducer by observing when the peak of the arch appears. But, this still doesn't mean its tail is directly beneath your transducer.

A narrowing of the whiteline on a graph will indicate you are passing over a soft spot in the bottom as mentioned previously. On flasher units (or graphs not sporting the whiteline feature), you can uncover changes in the bottom composition by observing the second echo reading. (Remember how important that second echo reading is.) Passing over soft bottom will make the second echo fade away or disappear completely. Hard bottom, rocks and gravel, or an old roadbed will generate sharp, bright multiple bottom echoes. Soft bottom absorbs; hard bottom reflects. That's a little information that may help when you're searching for the best location to string your trotline, ambush a sauger or entice a hungry smallmouth.

You may not have a memory like a filing cabinet, and all this information may take a while to fully soak in. But, even more important, you might need a little help initially building confidence in your depthfinder. Just because the unit says that the bottom is 36 feet under your hull, how do you know it isn't lying? Take a measured line and test it. Your depthfinder could have a couple of cross-eyed circuits, or maybe something that makes the wheels spin out of sync. Use a measured line to prove your unit is telling the truth about the bottom depth. If that checks out, you can trust the rest of the information. Confidence in your depthfinder makes it much easier to use it effectively.

The "marker button" on some graph units can be used as an aid in reconstructing water situations and locations when you are at home reviewing the day's progress on the chart paper. All the button does is draw a solid, black line down the width of the paper. But, you can use one line to indicate point A, two lines to indicate point B, and so forth. Work out your own code system, and use a pencil to record other important information on the chart paper for future reference. In this manner, you can build a fine fishing library of the action you encounter on the lake day after day. It doesn't matter whether you fish tournaments or try to fill the family freezer, that record can be valuable the next year when you return to the same spot at the same time of year. With a little luck from the weatherman and Mother Nature, fish will be in the same place at the same time, year after year. And, they probably will hit the same lures if you care to record that, also.

Operating a depthfinder properly comes with practice and time spent on the water. With serious practice, and serious hours spent on the water reading your sonar equipment signals, you can learn to understand the information your unit provides. It will be your own desire to learn and the amount of time you devote to the learning process that determines how far you can go with sonar.

5

Interpreting The Signal

nterpreting sonar signals is tough because everything keeps changing in water. Temperature, clarity, algae levels, fish movements, even the season of the year will alter what you see displayed on your sonar flasher or graph. Regardless of the time of year or the species of fish you seek, one thing will remain constant: You will, without fail, see something on the face of your unit which you don't completely understand!

Among experts and beginners alike, while watching the running depthfinder, the most often asked question is, "What the heck is that?" This chapter deals with how to interpret the signals you see on your sonar equipment. Before getting into the nuts and bolts of sonar interpretation, two statements should be made:

There is absolutely no substitute for personal experience in building your expertise for interpreting sonar signals. And ...

Nobody can interpret accurately every single mark or flash on a depthfinder.

As you read this chapter, please keep in mind that the following comments are made on the assumption that you have installed your transducer correctly, and have learned how to operate the controls on your depthfinder with some degree of efficiency. Otherwise, these comments on how to interpret signals correctly will not be valid.

Starting Fresh With Sonar

The first time you leave the dock with a new depthfinder in-

When you're using your depthfinder for the first time, it can be a little confusing. However, it will become easier with time, and help you take fish like this.

Interpreting The Signal

Thoroughly studying graph paper from your latest fishing trip is fine, but it's better if you can correlate the charts with a good topographical map of the lake you were fishing.

stalled in your boat, be ready for a surprise when you turn on the switch. You will most likely begin seeing all sorts of things beneath the surface almost immediately.

Don't worry. At that speed, there is nothing wrong with your unit. You can bet your gas money that the objects appearing on your sonar display are really down there—hundreds of them.

The trick is to figure out what all those images represent. Some of them are baitfish; others are gamefish. The "Christmas tree" light-up is probably just that: an underwater treetop. That single image displayed momentarily was probably a lonesome bass or a misguided crappie away from its friends.

A topographical map of the lake will prove most helpful when you begin "fishing" with 12 volts. Professionals use these things to find structure whenever possible, and you can do the same with your map. At this point, forget about fishing for the moment and concentrate on finding various types of underwater structure to look over. Steer the boat toward a sloping point which goes out into the lake from the shoreline. Move back and forth across it, watching how the depthfinder signals come up gradually from the bottom, bounce around a bit while you're over the top of the point, and then taper back down slowly as you move across the far side. Observe how the bottom signals widen slightly as you go over the edge of the point. This is because your signal cone is recording the bottom at more than one depth along the slope simultaneously. That bouncing around business while you're on top of the point (or slightly off to one side) is probably due to some stumps or brush there.

Continue using the map to find underwater trees, stump rows, old river channels and sharp drop-offs. Each will produce a distinctive signal on your depthfinder. You may not be able to recognize it at first, but keep running the boat over these things and let the signals soak into your memory banks. Put away the map and cruise to another part of the lake. Check the signals you see and try to identify the type of underwater structure below. Then, take a peek at the map to see if you were correct. When you can identify various types of bottom structure fairly accurately, you are ready for the next step.

One thing you may notice when fishing with an angler who has a depthfinder in his boat is that frequently he cannot put the boat over the same spot twice in a row. He motors along searching for fish until something promising pops up on the depthfinder. Then he says, "Hey! There they are!" and cuts the throttle back. He eases the boat around, goes back to where he thinks the fish are, and the depthfinder shows a blank. Granted, sometimes the boat will spook fish when it passes over them. But, most of the time, the boat operator simply cannot return to the same spot. Wind, current or a pure lack of any real sense of direction can make the task more complicated, but it isn't all that easy to go back to the exact same spot on the water where the fish signals were seen.

Practice, Practice, Practice

Find a reasonably large piece of structure on the bottom which juts upward. A single big stump, a solitary treetop or a large boul-

This is an excellent spot for practicing with your all-important depthfinder. Locate a piece of structure that is highly noticeable and practice finding it time and time again.

der. Anything unusual which stands out on the bottom will do for this exercise.

Find the piece of structure (a large stump, for example) and maneuver the boat over it. Then, practice turning slowly so you don't spook the stump, and steering the boat right back onto the target, stopping when the stump is directly beneath your boat. You will find that this critically important ability is much more difficult than you might imagine. You will also need a rather generous frustration quotient before mastering the technique. It's like the man said about hitting the center of a 100-yard rifle target, "There's a lot of space all around the bull's-eye!" There's a lot of water all around that stump, too. And, if you're a few feet off to one side or the other when you come back by, you'll never see it.

Many fishermen use floating marker buoys to simplify the task.

Complete Angler's Library

This is fine, but the average fish probably doesn't care much for having a heavy lead weight dropped on its head just so you can find the right spot again. This is especially true of bass and stripers that routinely swim away from large falling weights. In this case, you can return to the exact spot again, but the fish will probably not be there.

You may find it handy to develop the habit of noting a few landmarks when you pass over fish. By making mental notes like: "the big red oak was lined up with the little green pop can on the bank," you can ease the frustration of putting your boat back where you want it. Out in open water where landmarks are more elusive, you can drop a marking buoy a boat-length beyond where the fish are spotted. Then, on your return, go past the marker the appropriate distance, and look for your fillets. It helps to remember which side of the school you dropped the marker on.

As you begin to get a clear idea of how various bottom structures appear on your depthfinder, you will be ready to start work on the objects which appear somewhere between the top and bottom of the lake. Mid-depth readings are usually "where the action is" on sonar. A lake of average fertility will produce literally thou-

Recognizing fish on your depthfinder is only half the battle. By the time you've spotted the fish and stopped your boat, you're already past them. You will need to return to that same spot on the water.

Interpreting The Signal

sands of mid-depth readings for you to enjoy, and decipher.

Reading Fish Signals

If you have a fair understanding of fish habitat, you should have an easier time when you go fishing. Years ago, some people thought largemouth bass were invented by the U.S. Army Corps of Engineers. Today, we know this is not true. Stumps, logs and drop-offs invented them. As a bonus, they invented bream, catfish, crappie and muskies, too. With this firmly in mind, you must understand that different types of fish will relate to different types of structure, water temperature, depth and so forth. Then, when the winter comes, they pack their pebbles and vacation in somebody else's home.

This business of finding fish in relation to structure (habitat) is pretty much a proven fact, with the possible exception of carp. There have been suspicions that people with an affinity for carp fishing would rather spend their money on doughballs than depthfinders. This could be wrong. For example, you might spot a big fish sitting alone out in the middle of the lake well away from any structure. If so, you might wager it's a carp. This is because most anglers think that no self-respecting bass would ever consider commuting.

If you plan to use sonar signals to find gamefish living around structure in a lake, it follows you should be able to tell the difference between trees and fish scales, right? Otherwise, you'll end up fishing in a "school" of tree branches, much to the disgust of your depthfinder. In order to learn how to see fish and tell them from structure, you should purchase a few dozen small jigs.

Choose jigs or grubs in a style and size popular on your particular lake, ones known to take a variety of species such as bass, bream, crappie and white bass. You probably will lose most of your jig inventory to treetops at first, so pop for the cost of several cards of them. You can maximize the fun you are about to have by using ultra-light tackle.

Tie on a jig and go hunting at mid-depth for a strong sonar signal. Either drop over a marker buoy on the spot, or use your hard-won skills to return the boat to the spot of the signal. When you see the signal again on your unit, work the jig down there until you catch whatever it happens to be.

Maybe it will be a treetop, and you'll lose the jig. If so, take a

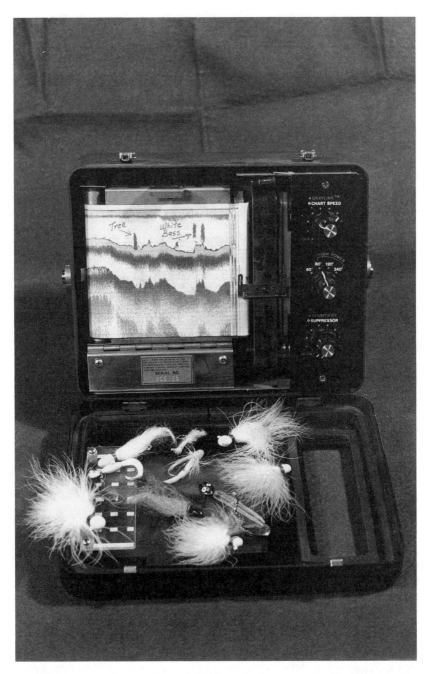

Jigs and sonar seem to go together well. While you're learning to identify different species through screen patterns, you can confirm your suspicions by dropping a jig over the boat's side and catching one for verification.

Interpreting The Signal

A benefit of using chart paper is being able to write notes on the paper next to the signal. This helps you remember exactly what that particular signal meant.

close look at how that treetop actually appears on your flasher or graph. If you are using a paper graph, write the word "treetop" by the image. If you are using a flasher, do your best to remember how the thing looks in lights. The same procedure applies if you catch a white bass, crappie, bream or whatever. Write the word, or remember what the signals look like if you can. Sometimes, the signals will be from a school of shad, and you will end up not catching anything.

The learning process for mid-depth image interpretation is greatly enhanced if you have a paper graph. You can write all over the paper as you go, and you can keep it for reference and comparisons. After several rolls of paper have been burned in the process, you will begin to observe patterns in the behavior of various species of fish. You will note that trees are usually attached to the

Complete Angler's Library

bottom of the lake and that shad bunch so tightly together in a school that they appear as a solid mass. (They look that way on a flasher, too.) Crappies seem to school in a somewhat horizontal formation, while white bass may position themselves in schools vaguely resembling the shape of a Christmas tree (when they aren't feeding on the surface). Largemouth bass, walleye and salmon form schools much more loosely, and individual "hooks or arched images are drawn for each fish on the paper. You can't miss the stripers because of their size.

These observations may not always enable you to identify correctly the species of every school of fish you see on your depthfinder. But, by using small jigs to catch and identify the things you see on your sonar equipment, you'll eliminate many hours spent wondering and asking, "What the heck is that?"

6

Fine-Tuning
Interpretation Skills

Most sonar operators never progress beyond the basics you have just read. In fact, some would be delighted with the ability to just identify a treetop when they see it on a screen. It takes dedication if you hope to use sonar signals to the fullest extent possible in your fishing.

If you have spent the required time learning the basic interpretation skills previously covered, and can identify bottom structure, treetops and suspended schools of fish, and if you are willing to spend a lot more time learning through personal experience, then you're ready to proceed to more advanced sonar-reading techniques.

Candidly, what you read here will have to be fortified with your own experience on the water before much of it will become clear to you, anyway. You should take one situation at a time from the several which follow, and try to duplicate it several times before proceeding to the next one.

Bottom Composition

Remembering the basic principles of sonar, you know that hard surfaces reflect more of your unit's signal than do softer ones. As the transducer passes over a rocky bottom, the flasher signal will become noticeably wider and more intense (brighter). The correct bottom depth remains at the top of the signal on the dial. On graph units, the bottom also expands, again only in a downward fashion. If your graph has a grayline feature, you will notice

Learning to interpret sonar signals is not an easy task. The only way to enhance your skills is to get out on the water. Personal experience and practice will help you develop into a more successful sonar user ... and angler.

Fine-Tuning Interpretation Skills   87

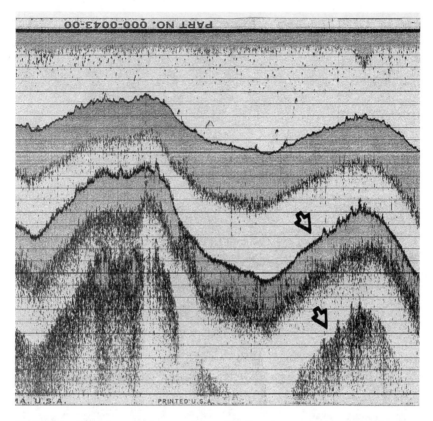

With the depthfinder's sensitivity control properly adjusted, you can record multiple echoes while passing over a hard bottom. This is why you don't want to have the sensitivity set too low.

that the shaded area extends farther down on the paper, indicating a hard bottom below. A second or even third bottom echo will appear on both units, provided the sensitivity is set properly and there is sufficient room on the graph paper.

Finding an old roadbed hideout for your quarry becomes "a piece of cake" with this knowledge. Finding a submerged weedbed or moss bed is equally easy when you think about it. The signals weaken substantially when they are being partially absorbed by the vegetation, and the second echo disappears.

Gravel, rock, mud, sand and moss bottoms are all fairly easy to pick out with practice when you watch the returning bottom signals get wider or weaker. Even very slight changes in bottom composition will be shown plainly by the action of the second echo. The second bottom echo is much weaker than the first one, so it

Complete Angler's Library

will be affected more by changes in the strength of reflected signals than the initial reading. That's important to remember, especially with flasher units.

Drop-Offs

An uneven bottom which climbs or drops irregularly beneath the boat will generate a wide returning signal on a flasher. Actually, it is returning several bottom signals all at once because there are a variety of depths to choose from while the cone moves over the drop-off. Not being picky, the depthfinder will display all of them for you within the cone from the transducer. Very steep drop-offs show themselves in very wide bottom readings; gradual slopes or drop-offs produce only slightly enlarged bottom readings.

Nice, smooth slopes on the bottom with no breaks and brush will appear as a solid line, but rocky drop-offs will return nervous signals for bottom readings, bouncing the sound waves all around the place, ricocheting in every direction. Drop-offs featuring stumps, brush and irregular structural formations will return broken bottom readings, too.

A flasher can mislead you under these circumstances if you fail to realize what is going on down there. When the transducer is positioned over a slope, especially a steep one, the center of the cone is shooting and receiving signals which strike the bottom at different depths. However, the edge of that cone is weaker than the center with regard to signals. Frequently, there seems to be a small, weaker signal hovering just above the main bottom readings at the most shallow point. It looks very much like a fish signal. Usually, it is not.

The single, weaker signal displayed immediately above the bottom readings on a slope is probably an additional returning signal from the bottom. It comes from the outer edge of the cone slightly farther up the hillside, and looks like a fish hovering there. This type of false reading happens only on a drop-off, and only when the slope is reasonably sharp. When you run over a flat bottom with your flasher unit, the outer edge signals will appear merged into the main bottom reading, although they actually show up *below* the correct depth.

Finally, even the real experts with sonar equipment cannot readily identify fish holding along the bottom on a rocky drop-off. The fish signals simply merge into the bottom reading. Turning

Fine-Tuning Interpretation Skills

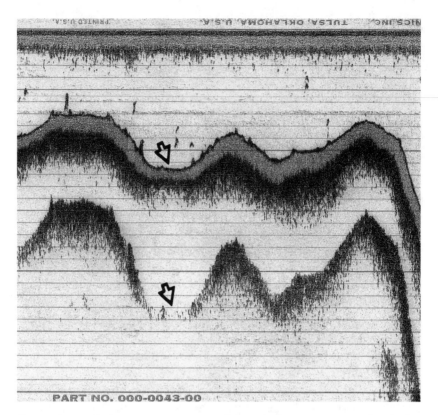

Your unit's second echo is more sensitive to small changes in bottom composition than the first one. As this boat passed over the softer section of bottom, the grayline narrows slightly; however, the second echo disappears completely.

the sensitivity either "up" or "down" does not help because of the stronger signals from the hard, rocky bottom.

There is a slight chance you will be able to spot fish under these conditions, but only if they are moving. Then, if there is no wind or current and the boat doesn't move, it follows the signals which pass through the cone are probably coming from restless fish. Bottom signals will remain reasonably steady, excluding the little false return. The weak bottom signal which hovers above the drop-off will be much less intense than fish signals, although signals from both may come and go.

It's really not worth all that time and effort to remain frozen over a rocky drop-off waiting for a fish to swim under the boat. If you want to find the presence of fish on the drop, use one of those small jigs. Rocks don't eat jigs the same way fish do.

Brush, Trees And Weeds

Even experienced sonar operators sometimes get fooled, causing them to waste time fishing treetops which looked like fish on the screen. Many times, the signals displayed, especially on a flasher, can look alike.

As a general rule, you can count on trees and brush to be attached to the bottom. Signals for this type of structure normally begin at the bottom reading and continue upward in a broken pattern until they reach the top of the underwater object. Unfortunately, it doesn't work exactly like that every time on flashers or graphs.

Even with the best sonar units, tall underwater trees can be displayed as if they are free-floating in the water as the boat passes overhead. The only logical explanation for this would be that a

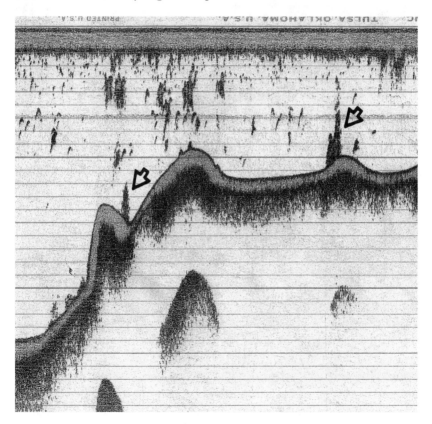

Typical images produced from signals returning from underwater trees will appear to be firmly attached to the bottom, as indicated by the arrows.

Sometimes, "tree" images will appear to be floating in the water. This may be because the tree's upper-most limbs are blocking signals, preventing them from reaching the tree's lower portion.

mass of limbs and branches is extending out from the tree trunk and has the effect of blocking some of the signals either going from or returning to the transducer. The unit isn't receiving returning signals from the tree trunk under the canopy so it displays nothing there, even though the tree obviously is attached to the bottom. Increasing the sensitivity level on the unit may cause the tree trunk to appear if you really need to see it.

In this situation, you will get a complete bottom reading because of the signals being sent and returned along the edge of the cone. The way a depthfinder displays images makes it appear you are getting a bottom reading directly under the "suspended" tree when you actually are not. As a result, the depthfinder shows an accurate reading for the top two-thirds of the tree, but perhaps shows nothing for the lower portion of the trunk because no signals traveled that far. In addition, it may show a slightly deeper bottom reading than the actual bottom depth.

This can be proven by carefully watching the signals reflected from a tree as you approach it on the water. When the tree is first hit by signals along the forward edge of your cone, the angle is better for allowing the signals to work in under some of the branches. You probably observe the tree attached or nearly attached to the bottom. Then, as you continue to move directly above the tree, the object seems to move up in depth slightly toward you. It looks as if it took a deep breath and floated up a few feet or yards!

Turning up the sensitivity can sometimes provide a top-to-bottom reading in these cases, depending on just how tightly massed the limbs are and how much moss is growing on them. Luckily, most of the trees in your lake should provide a complete reading, appearing firmly planted onto the bottom.

Using the basics of sonar interpretation will allow you to pull off some pretty nifty tricks with which to impress your fishing partner. For example, you can spot fish holding *inside* the branches of a treetop if you're alert enough. Signals reflected from hard surfaces are more intense than signals from soft surfaces, right? So, if you are over a treetop and the unit's sensitivity is turned down, the weak signals from soft, water-soaked branches will fade out. The stronger signals from fish holding there will remain! Turn down the sensitivity until the tree signals almost disappear completely. The remaining, strong signals should be fish. Of course, getting those fish out of that treetop and into your boat is another problem!

Weeds extending up from the bottom will return weaker, paler signals than practically any other type of surface. Again, using the basics, you should be able to see fish holding in the weedbeds easily. No adjustment of sensitivity will be required for that one.

Phase Three

A few other advanced techniques need to be examined in learning about sonar equipment. NAFC Members will find that with time and experience their depthfinders will become the most valuable tool for finding fish. As an angler continues working with these units on the water, and sharpening skills for interpreting

This angler identified the thermocline on his graph, and made his presentation at the correct depth. The result was a nice stringer of stripers.

what the signals represent, he will become more aware of subtle differences, small details never seen before, and a host of little things which are puzzling.

Some of today's more expensive and sophisticated graphs have an amazing capacity for showing these small readings. By judicious use of the sensitivity control, you can determine at what depth the thermocline is located. As indicated in other Complete Angler's Library volumes, the thermocline is the most productive layer of water for fishing under most conditions. Above it is the epilimnion, or surface layer of water which absorbs heat from the sun; below is the hypolimnion, a layer of water with very low oxygen content, usually devoid of fish life.

The reason your graph can identify the thermocline's location is that there is a rather abrupt temperature change between layers in the water. Sudden temperature changes in the water are accompanied by changes in density. It is the change in water density that is recorded by these sophisticated units, providing a picture of the fish's "comfort zone." That information can be used to your advantage.

A few errors, or at least illusions, are built into the sonar readout you see. Fish which can be seen anywhere within the transducer's circular cone of sound will appear on the unit's face as if they were directly beneath the boat. Actually, only a few fish swimming within a given circle will be exactly in the center of that circle. Most of the fish you see displayed on the sonar screen will be off to one side or the other within the cone, not directly under the transducer as they appear to be. For this reason, most fish will be from 5 to 10 percent closer to the water's surface than they seem to be on the screen.

Fish (or other underwater objects) directly under the transducer will be recorded accurately on your depthfinder at their exact depth. If the object is near the edge of the sound cone, thereby being farther away in signal distance from the transducer, it will appear to be at a greater depth because of the additional time it

Stratification And The Thermocline

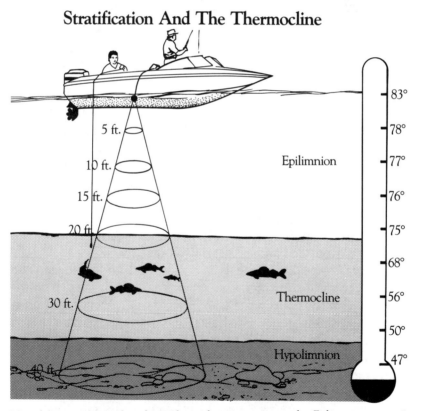

Many lakes stratify into three distinct layers during summer months. Fishermen are most interested in the thermocline layer. It provides water temperatures most fish prefer.

Fine-Tuning Interpretation Skills

takes for the signal to make its roundtrip.

Perhaps the easiest way to understand this is to study the hooked, or "arched" symbols that are drawn on a graph. When a suspended fish first enters a moving transducer's circle of sound waves, it is at its farthest distance from the transducer. When the unit begins recording that signal, the fish is on the outer edge of the cone. As the boat's approach continues, the echo signal returns in less time because the fish is closer to the cone's center. This is why an arch is drawn for a fish on your graph. The signal starts at a lower depth and moves upward as you move over it. Even though the depth at which the fish is holding doesn't change, the linear distance to the fish has decreased, so the signal prints closer to the surface. As you pass over the fish, the peak is reached, and the line heads downward until the fish passes out of the sound cone.

The fish's *actual* depth will be the highest point of the arch—if the transducer passes directly over the fish. Even if it doesn't, we're talking in terms of a difference of only a matter of inches if you are fishing in most freshwater lakes. But, there is a practical advantage to knowing this.

On the graph, you can quickly determine if the fish you see is right under the boat or if it is off to one side. This "fine point" in interpretation can make a substantial difference when you're vertically jigging for tightly bunched, suspended fish. The sharper the arch, the closer the fish is to being directly under the transducer. The lazy, gentle arches you see are caused by fish passing through the cone's outer edges. These signals are more rounded in appearance on the graph because position relative to the transducer doesn't change as much. Sharp arches mean fish under the transducer. Rounded arches mean fish off to the side.

Generally speaking, the larger the depthfinder image, the larger the fish it is showing. This holds true for a single fish swimming through the transducer's cone. But, when two or more fish are swimming close together, their signals may merge, resulting in a "larger than life" image. Also, when two or more fish are passing beneath your transducer at the same depth, although they may be several feet apart horizontally, the unit may record their signals as one. Signals are blended and merged into one because the fish are at the same depth. (This is especially true with flasher units.)

Another funny-looking image which frequently pops up on

graphs is a thin, straight vertical line (often seeming to float in the water). The recorded signal, looking as if you just passed over a vertically floating telephone pole, can stretch for several feet in height as shown on the chart paper. Sometimes this phenomenon is represented by a series of small arches stacked one on top of the other in a vertical column several feet deep. As no variety of man nor fish stacks itself tightly in single file vertically underwater, what could this signal represent on your graph? Air bubbles or gas rising from the bottom seems to be the only reasonable answer.

Conclusions

Nothing can replace personal experience in gaining the expertise to read sonar signals properly. Expertise comes only after long hours of serious study on the water.

You cannot bolt on a depthfinder, run to the water and triple your fishing success immediately. Do not allow frustration to make you impatient. You will increase your fishing success dramatically as you gain this experience and apply it to your efforts in boating fish.

Learn to read bottom detail first. Use a topographical map as an aid whenever possible. When you can identify drop-offs, trees and underwater islands, begin working on fish signals. If you have a graph, always write notes on the paper explaining what you find. And, remember that small jigs are quite valuable in validating what you're learning to read from fish signals.

As you master the basics of interpretation, your personal skills and ingenuity will begin to surface in the learning process. You will build expertise with depthfinders in direct relation to the time and effort you are willing to expend. If you get too frustrated, go back to "square one" and review the basics.

You can master sonar interpretations—if you're dedicated.

Taking A Close Look

7

Liquid Crystal Graphs

Liquid Crystals, LCDs, LCGs—call them what you will. During the past few years this technology has found a permanent home in the angling world, and made loyal fans out of millions of anglers. Bass, crappie, striper, walleye and salmon anglers alike all have adopted these easy-to-use sonar devices for finding fish, no matter if they're hugging the bottom or riding high in the water column.

Acceptance of these new-generation sonar units wasn't always assured, however. In the early days, liquid crystal units were considered a gimmick by some—a fishfinder strictly for beginners, or for those who didn't take fishing very seriously. For *real* fishermen who were used to a flasher's instantaneous response or a paper graph's incredible ability to show detail, liquid crystals simply were too slow and showed too little detail. There simply were not enough "pixels" on the screen for more detailed pictures of fish, structure and the bottom's topography.

Thanks mainly to advancements in design but partly to anglers' increased awareness, liquid crystals are now the most popular type of sonar unit on the market. "Liquid crystal technology has improved tremendously," says Gary Roach, a well-known angler and National Fresh Water Fishing Hall-of-Famer. "It used to be that a die-hard flasher user like me wouldn't think of depending on liquid-crystal sonar. But, with the technology available today, you can run any structure you want to and pick fish right off the bottom."

LCG units have become extremely dominant in the sportfishing market. It's difficult to find other types of sonar units in tackle shops.

If there's a downside to the liquid crystal's success as a fishfinding tool and its resulting popularity, it may be that it comes at the expense of anglers who also like to run flasher units. LCGs have dominated the market to the extent that flashers have disappeared from store shelves and the pages of fishing catalogs. Many flasher fanatics bought two or three units before the supply vanished to assure the continued use of their favorite type of sonar for many years.

LCG Basics

LCD (liquid crystal display) and LCG (liquid crystal graph) have long been used interchangeably to describe liquid crystal sonar equipment. But lately, LCG has emerged as the favorite, probably because these display screens most commonly offer information to the angler in a form similar to that of a paper graph. Some units, however, allow the angler to switch the screen from a "graph" to a "flasher" display with the flip of a toggle switch. At least one unit has a split-screen feature that allows the angler to view both a liquid crystal flasher *and* graph.

Although an LCG is different in appearance from a paper graph or flasher, it's really quite similar in operation. Just like a paper graph or flasher, an LCG generates electrical energy that is sent to the transducer, which converts it into sound energy. Following basic sonar principles, those sound waves travel through the water, bounce off the bottom (or objects) and are picked up by the unit's receiver on the return trip. The unit calculates distance to the bottom or an object by the amount of time it takes for the sound waves to leave the transducer and return. The only difference in the operation of an LCG is the manner in which it displays that information—on a liquid crystal display screen.

Liquid crystal is one of those substances that frustrates the high-school science student who's been taught that everything falls into one of three categories: solid, liquid or gas. Liquid crystal, however, seems to be one of the exceptions. It flows like a liquid, but has the molecular makeup of a solid. Without becoming bogged down by scientific details, just think of it as a liquid solution in which tiny crystals are suspended.

These crystals are rod-like in shape, and respond to many types of forces, including an electrical charge, by changing position. Hold a pencil between your thumb and forefinger so that it points away from you. Close one eye and you will see only the end of the pencil. Now, turn your fingers 90 degrees so that you see the length of the pencil. This is how liquid crystals move when manipulated by an electrical charge.

In an LCG, there are three pieces of glass. The liquid crystal solution is pressed between two sheets of glass, and a piece of polarized glass is on top. One of the glass sheets that traps the liquid crystal is etched in a cross-hatch pattern with conductive material deposited along the etching. These tiny squares are the basis of the pixels (tiny square segments) you see on the screen. When the sonar's processor determines that a certain pixel should be charged, electrical current is sent to that square etched in the glass and the crystal rods within that square turn. The polarized glass on top of the stack makes it appear that the pixel has turned black.

Liquid Crystals: How They Work

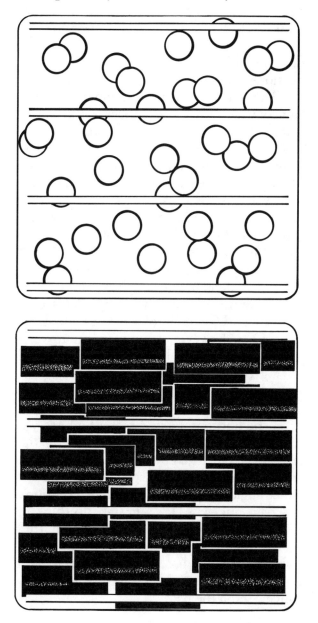

Rod-shaped liquid crystals, when not in use (top), allow light to pass from a reflecting surface to the angler's eyes. When charged with electricity, these rods turn to block the light (bottom), making the pixel appear black.

In reality, the crystals involved have simply turned lengthwise, blocking the light from a reflector behind the sandwich. These darkened pixels create the images that appear on the screen.

Pixel Counts And Resolution

As mentioned before, pixels are arranged in a grid pattern on the screen. The screen is a certain number of pixels high and a certain number wide. While the number of pixels on the horizontal axis is important to the amount of bottom "history" you can see on the screen, the vertical line of pixels is critical to how much resolution the unit offers. What is resolution? Think back to the very first LCGs to hit the market. Their screen had only 50 to 60 pixels on the vertical axis.

That meant that, in 60 feet of water, each of the 50 vertical pixels represented a little more than 14 inches of depth. Two fish suspended within that distance of each other would show up as a single blob on the screen. Likewise, a fish less than 14 inches off the bottom would blend in with the bottom on the screen. That was the biggest drawback with the early LCGs—one that made serious anglers view LCG technology with some skepticism.

Modern LCGs, however, have many more vertical pixels. High-resolution units usually have around 128, with the top-end models having 200. These LCGs can delineate individual fish only inches apart, even in deep water. More vertical pixels means better screen resolution.

Pixels on the horizontal axis represent a history of what the boat has passed over. The most up-to-date information of what's under the boat is represented by the vertical row of pixels on the extreme right-hand side of the display. And, one of the biggest mistakes some anglers make is focusing their attention on the center of the screen. Likewise, it's a mistake to think that a wide-screen LCG shows a wider view of the bottom. In truth, it shows only a longer history of what the boat has passed over. If you want to know what's under the boat *now*, concentrate on the images appearing at the right side of the screen. Everything else you see is some distance behind the boat.

LCG Advantages

In addition to advancements in its ability to show detail, why have LCGs become so popular among all types of anglers? There

LCGs And Resolution

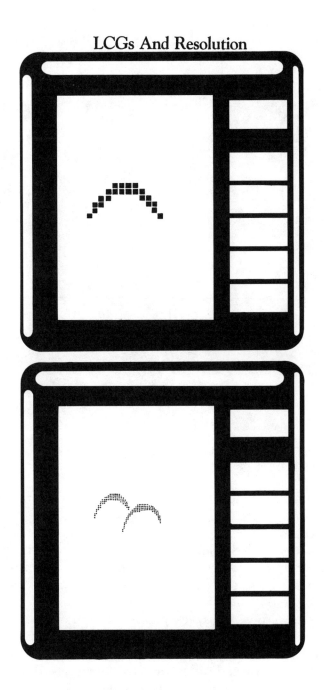

Earlier LCG models with fewer vertical pixels, such as 30 or 60 (top), cannot create a display showing individual fish close to each other. Newer units with 200 vertical pixels (bottom) provide a more defined picture of the world below the boat.

LCG sonar makes fishing a breeze. Its automatic functions free your hands for fighting fish. If you prefer a more detailed display, switch it to the manual mode.

are many reasons. One is that they offer the angler information in the same sort of "picture" form as supplied by a paper graph, but without the hassle or expense of having to change paper. But, that's a double-edged fillet knife, as well. Because there is no graph paper, the angler does not have a permanent record of what happened on the water. That alone, to some anglers, is reason enough to avoid LCGs.

LCGs are also very easy to operate. They allow the angler to choose between operating the unit in either its manual or automatic mode. When set to operate automatically, the machine selects the depth range and will adjust sensitivity levels. But, whether the feature is really something that you would use depends upon your skill as angler and sonar operator. If you're a serious fisherman, you'll probably use your LCG most often in the manual mode, fine-tuning the controls yourself to get the best possible picture. You don't want to miss a single clue that may reveal the appearance of bottom structure, or where a fish might be holding.

If you're more relaxed about your fishing, the automatic mode is probably the way to go. The unit decides which depth range to focus on and at what sensitivity level to operate. Granted, an LCG set to operate automatically will almost certainly offer a picture that's a tad less detailed. But, if your primary goal is to have fun, rather than trying to pinpoint every fish in the lake, an LCG set on automatic will help you achieve it.

Another major advantage that LCGs have over paper graphs and flashers is that they're totally electronic. They contain no motors, and thus no moving parts. In fact, unless you accidentally drop your anchor on top of it, your LCG is nearly indestructible.

Because it's entirely electronic, with delicate inner workings, corrosion is the only real enemy an LCG has. Fortunately, manufacturers seal the units at the factory, locking out moisture. They're so well sealed that they would actually float if dropped over the side of the boat. Still, there's one factor that requires caution when buying an LCG. Make sure it's one that has been filled with nitrogen before being sealed. Manufacturers of quality LCGs make it a practice. If they didn't, the unit would contain air from the factory at whatever the moisture level was on the day it was sealed. Sooner or later that moisture would condense and corrode the electronics. The nitrogen forces the moisture-ladened air out of the unit.

LCG's Flip Side

So far, the LCG would seem to be the perfect sonar system for any circumstance. They do have their drawbacks, however, and for whatever reason, there's a certain number of anglers who would choose a flasher or paper graph over an LCG every time.

Among the minor negatives is the complaint that an LCG screen can be difficult to read sometimes, especially during low-light periods. Manufacturers reduced the problem a few years ago, however, when they introduced the "super twist" display. It was actually an improvement of the liquid crystal material itself. They found a way to make the crystals react to the electric charge better than before, making them more efficient light-blockers. That results in more contrast and better visibility on the screen.

This LCG unit provides superior visibility. It has a curved face plate to reduce glare and advanced signal processing. With its five display modes and continuous digital depth and depth scale readouts, it offers many advantages to anglers.

Operating an LCG in cold weather is also a trick. Low temperatures make the liquid crystal molecules react more slowly to the electric charge. Here again, LCG makers claim vast improvements in this area, but many anglers are inclined to disagree.

In that same vein, some anglers accuse LCGs of being just too slow, overall. Unlike a flasher that instantaneously shows you whatever's on the bottom, LCGs must first process the information before displaying it. The drawback is most evident, and can be most *dangerous*, when you're approaching an area with a quick-rising bottom at moderate to high speeds. The LCG may go blank while the unit tries to catch up to the information being received.

LCGs Of Tomorrow

There's no telling where LCG technology will head from

here. Indeed, manufacturers have already departed from what you would call "normal" displays. Since the first units were introduced, manufacturers have experimented with screens that used red pixels to identify which marks on the screen represented fish. Others have introduced machines that are only supposed to mark the species of fish you preselect, while others have built machines that provide anglers a three-dimensional view of the bottom and the fish's relation to structure.

As long as LCG researchers continue to have good imaginations, anglers can expect these sonar units to keep improving.

8

Graph Paper Interpretation

everal examples of chart paper which illustrate points previously covered in the text will be in this chapter. Most were burned with the unit set on the 60-foot scale, and each example should provide an opportunity for you to polish your reading and interpretation skills. (Try to figure out the main characters on the paper before reading the caption!) The examples apply to video images, too.

Included in sample charts (within this chapter) are curve-line graphs. If you're not familiar with this graph type, it can be difficult to interpret the information. However, it is worthwhile to know about the difference in "look."

There will be obvious differences in the way images appear on graphs from different manufacturers. No two manufacturers have graphs on the market which print or burn signals exactly alike. Don't let this bother you. Look for patterns, groupings and consistent displays of detail when comparing these examples to those you have run with your own unit.

The graph paper examples are from only one brand of unit, with few exceptions. This is not an indication of favoritism. If various brands had been used, the lack of similarity between the graph paper printouts could have been confusing. So, it is to your advantage that one brand is used.

While learning to interpret signal identifications, verify them, as well. This will help develop your interpretation skills more rapidly.

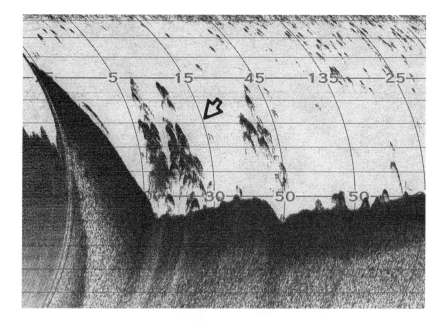

A large mass of fish (above) with medium separation (arrow) indicates a school of either crappies or white bass. The Christmas tree formation suggests white bass. Below, both fish groups are holding (arrows) inside a treetop. The fish echoes remain strong as the sensitivity level is decreased, allowing the tree to fade away.

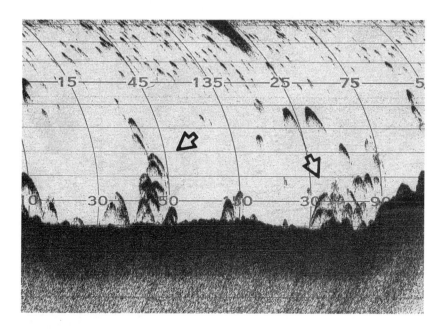

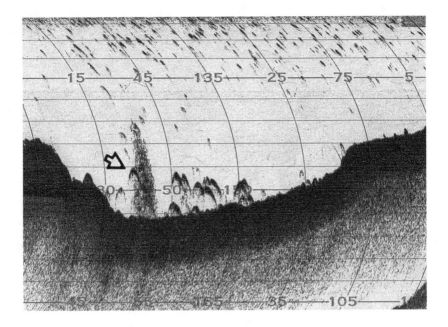

In the graph above, one bass is in the tree (arrow), while others begin to school more tightly together. (They're about to feed!) Below, fish on the left are loosely schooled over a large area, while the group at right is schooling more tightly, appearing to head for structure. Soon, they will be highly catchable.

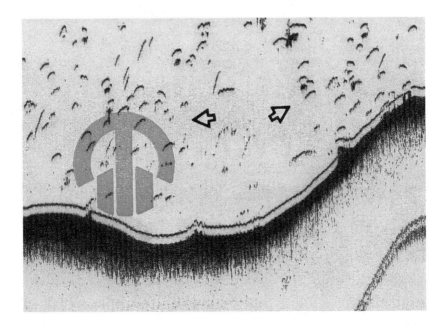

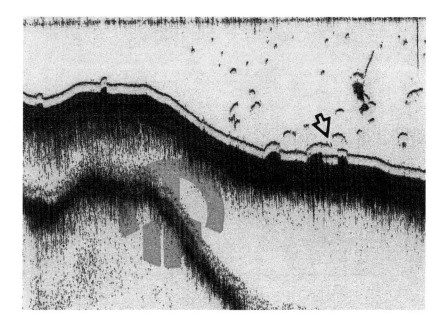

When the suppressor control isn't used (above) some graph units can display fish holding (arrow) almost on the bottom without the signals blending. (This fish is practically scratching his stomach on a stump.) When you find big stripers like this over a clean, snag-free bottom (below), it's time to break out the ultra-light tackle for some real excitement.

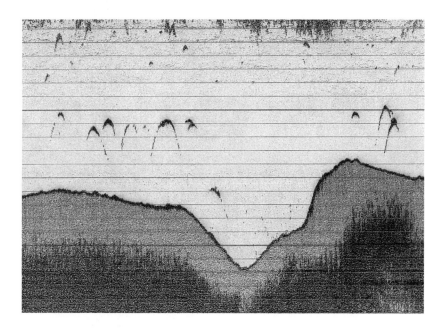

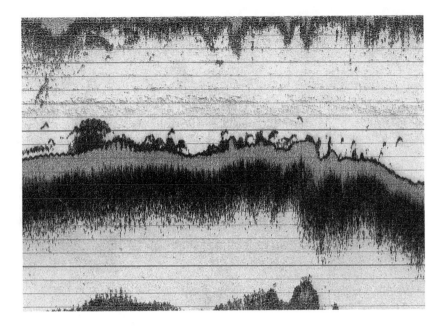

As indicated on this graph (above), the stumps and brush are home to many crappies. This scene (below) is a genuine fisherman's delight. As indicated on this graph, both ridges are filled with large, active fish. Now, all you have to do is find out what they like.

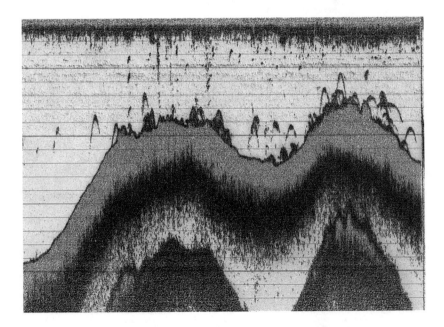

Bass suspend at depths that are comfortable for them when the lake has an oxygen problem *(above)*. They are considered active because they move directly over the structure when they begin feeding. This school is relating to an underwater hump *(arrows)*. Vertical jigging produced excellent results. A huge school of white bass *(below)* suspends just beneath the surface. Shad would be more tightly grouped, showing up as a solid mass.

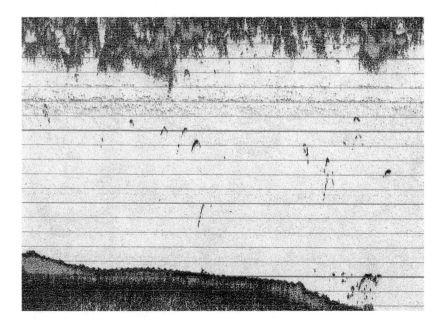

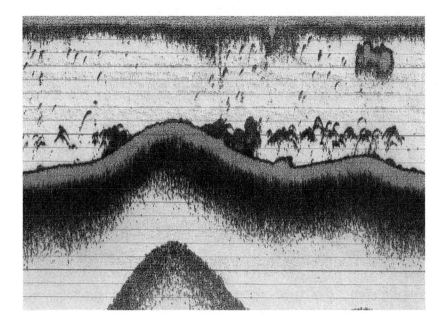

It would be difficult to find better action than this chart paper indicates (above). Good-sized fish are packed in on both sides of the ridge at about the same depth. Below, active bass attack everything in sight on both of these drop-offs. Fish signals are mixed with structure signals, indicating that the fish are feeding.

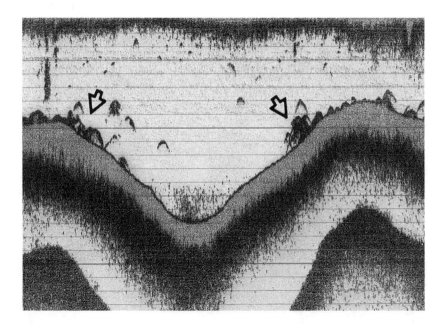

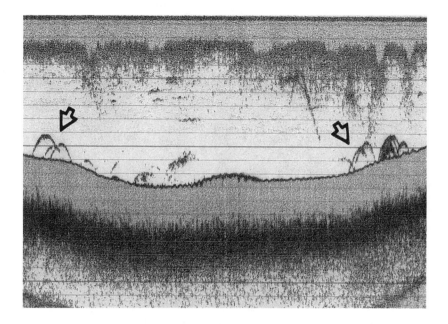

You can't miss the big stripers on this graph (above) because of their size. These stripers are on the bottom in 25 feet of water. Trolling for stripers in the early spring is a good way of filling your freezer. These stripers (below) are holding in about 17 feet of water.

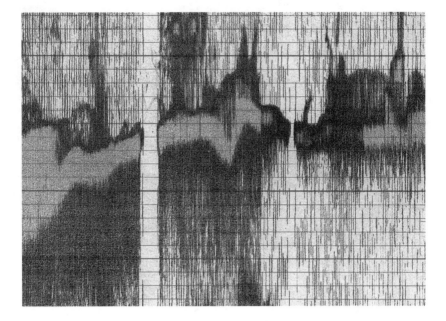

This (above) is a good example of what another unit will do to your chart recorder. It's time to tell Charlie to turn off the other unit. Excessive use of the suppressor control will blend signals together (below). Here, fish are holding tightly on the bottom, but the control is set too strong, resulting in fish signals (arrow) merging with bottom signals.

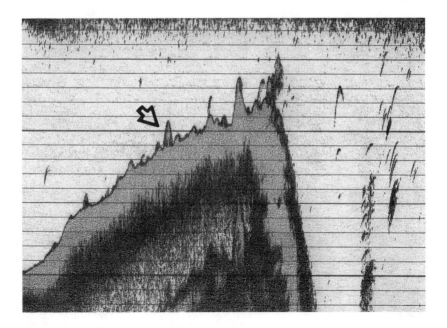

Complete Angler's Library

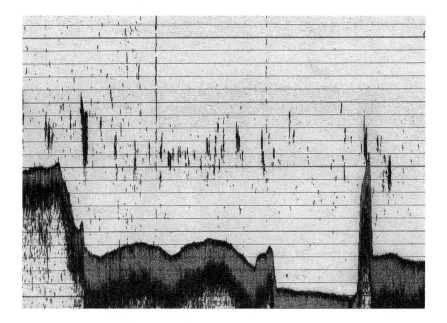

Your graph paper's travel speed (above) can make fish signals appear as straight, vertical lines. On the other hand (below), the combination of a fast paper speed and a very slow boat speed can result in fish signals being drawn as long, horizontal lines (arrow).

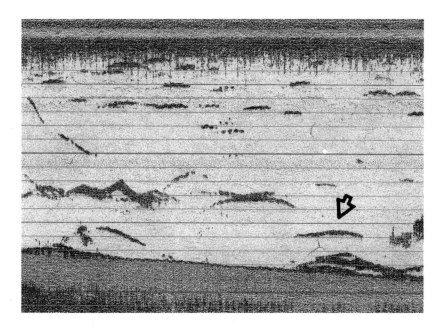

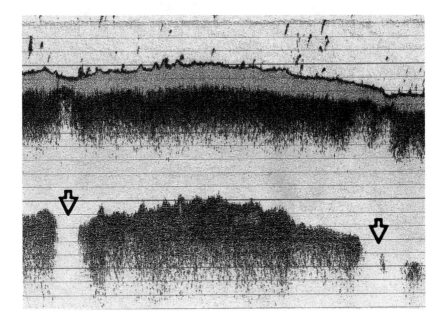

Even minor changes in bottom composition (above) will cause the grayline feature to narrow on the paper; the second bottom echo (arrows) will disappear. Some graph units (below) will show the thermocline layer (arrows) as a result of the sudden change in water density when the temperature drops. (Note absence of fish below this layer.)

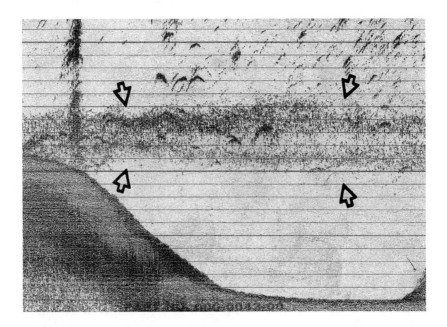

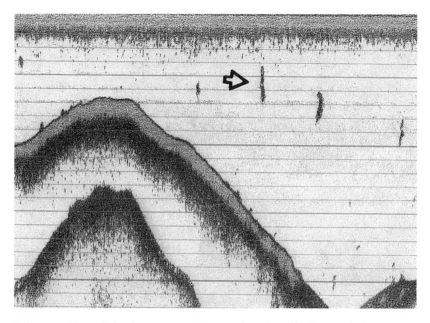

When vertically stacked arches appear in open space (as indicated by the arrow), they are most likely air bubbles.

Keep in mind while you study these sample graphs that no one can say with 100 percent certainty what fish it is that is represented on the graph paper. At best, interpreting is an educated guess. However, this is where experience and verification come into play. Unless you verify what the unit is telling you, you won't be able to develop a firm base of reliable information and experience to interpret the signals correctly.

Interpretation requires work and repeated experience on the water at different times of the year. This enables you to accurately identify different species by the way the symbols appear on the graph recorder. Then, you will start having more consistent success, and a lot more fun.

9

Maintenance And Troubleshooting Tips

E ven the very finest depthfinders on the market today are subject to failure sometime. And, the operator can cause the failure to happen prematurely by not taking a few common-sense precautions, and by not taking care of the unit properly. Like any sophisticated piece of circuitry, depthfinders can experience mechanical problems from wear, abuse or perhaps even a simple construction defect which slipped past the quality-control people at the plant. Regardless of how the problem occurs, the only time you will discover the fault is while you're on the water. And that is, of course, exactly when you need the unit to work!

Lost fishing time while the depthfinder is in the shop is certainly a problem. The repair bill after the warranty expires can be another source of frustration. There is little advantage to be gained by being careless in the area of depthfinder maintenance. The following suggestions for delaying or avoiding mechanical problems are worth heeding.

The owner's manual which accompanied your sonar machine home from the store should have some pertinent information on the subject of maintenance for your particular unit. Read the manual and follow the manufacturer's advice. However, the following tips may, or may not, have appeared in your manual.

Transducers
Your transducer is the "eye" for your entire sonar system. If it

Before even going on the water, you should carefully read the owner's manual that came with your particular sonar unit. Most manuals provide various maintenance tips. Remember, the best way to solve a problem is to prevent it.

Maintenance And Troubleshooting Tips 123

gets in trouble, nothing else works efficiently. The transducer contains a crystal which must be protected from sharp blows. If the site of the transducer is at the boat's stern on the outside of the transom, you should give special consideration to the potential problems of high-speed boat travel where there is the possibility of striking a floating object.

In a busy marina, transom-mounted transducers also are exposed to floating oil and gas residue. If you keep your boat in a slip at the marina, the potential for trouble is compounded materially. Oil which is allowed to remain on a transducer's face can coat the eye, decreasing your system's performance. In time, oil can blind the transducer, and it must be replaced. Road film from trailering the boat to and from the lake can coat the transducer, so can algae which builds up on it when the boat remains idle for long time periods.

The transducer face must be cleaned frequently if it is exposed to these hazards. Use a wash rag dipped in warm, soapy water to scrub the transducer face several times each season. *Do not* use harsh abrasives or "steel wool."

Transducers mounted inside the boat that shoot signals through the hull do not require so much attention. However, a poor mounting job, or a sharp rap on the hull beneath the transducer can cause a crack to appear under the puck. Examine the mount regularly for signs of separation because oil will seep under the surface if given the chance. If silicone was used in mounting the transducer, it can be eaten up rather quickly by petroleum products, so frequent inspections are mandatory. And, even though the transducer is attached securely to the hull with epoxy, the sump area should be cleaned annually to protect the transducer cord from harsh chemicals. (It doesn't hurt to leave a bar of Ivory soap in the sump.)

Electrical Connections

Maintenance of battery connections, and any other electrical connections which can affect the depthfinder, is vitally important. Actually, it's critical. If your unit is portable with self-contained batteries, they should be removed when the equipment is not in use to prevent corrosion from battery leakage. After the depthfinder is mounted permanently in the boat, check the battery connections frequently for early signs of corrosion. It's a good idea to develop the habit of checking the battery connections ev-

Proper maintenance of your electrical system cannot be over-emphasized. Cables and connections should be checked regularly for undue wear.

Maintenance And Troubleshooting Tips

Keeping your battery terminals clean is mandatory in order to avoid potential unnecessary problems. With a little effort and some sandpaper, minor corrosion buildup can be removed. Also, remember to coat the posts and connections with grease or petroleum jelly.

ery time you fill the boat's gas tank. And, during the off-season while the boat sits idle, check it every two or three weeks.

Remove and clean all connections as frequently as needed. Minor corrosion build-up problems can be removed efficiently with 400-grit sandpaper and a dedication for being thorough. Remove all traces of the problem-causing corrosion from battery terminal posts and wires that are attached to them. When the battery and connectors are genuinely clean and corrosion-free, coat them heavily with grease or petroleum jelly. Clean and grease the terminals every two or three months, especially in hot weather.

This may sound like too much attention to give battery connections—it isn't. A master sonar mechanic, operating one of the nation's largest depthfinder repair centers, says a surprising number of units have to be sent in for repairs because the users didn't take the time to clean and maintain the battery terminals!

When battery terminals are allowed to corrode and oxidize, he says, they will "float" electrically. Even when the connectors are clamped on tightly, they will "disconnect" electrically. Then, when the big engine on your boat is started and turns a few high rpm, it can create excessive volt "spikes." These spikes bypass the battery because of the corrosion and enter the circuitry of your depthfinder. This surge destroys transistors and circuits, making a trip to the repair center necessary. (Your depthfinder is not the only item in the boat which can be destroyed under these circumstances. CB radios, solid state ignitions and tachometers are also vulnerable.)

Corrosion can invade the unit's power plug, transducer jack, fuse holder or power cord splices, too. This will create poor readings for you at best, and unit failure at worse. Check and clean these potential trouble spots frequently.

The smooth shaft of your transducer plug-in is easy enough to clean with fine sandpaper. However, the gunk that forms inside the power plug can be tough to remove. Some power plugs can be disassembled for cleaning; most can't. (You will remove skin on your thumb and forefinger trying to twirl a rolled-up piece of sandpaper within the small confines of the plug interior.)

Your best bet for combating corrosion inside the power plug is to not let it happen. If you put the plug inside a small plastic bag, secured by a rubber band or little wire-tie strip, it will not be subjected to build-up when it's not in use. The bag offers protection, even if your boat must be left outside. Shooting WD-40 or LPS2 into the plug will also help.

Special Procedures For Graphs

Graph units generate dust (carbon) inside the case as images are burned onto the paper. This dust should be removed regularly. Holding the unit over your head and blowing into it will do little more than transfer a good bit of the dust from the unit into your eyes and hair. A better way would be to use a low-pressure air hose. Blow out the dust with the pressure hose, but be sure the compressed air doesn't contain water or oil. Hold the nozzle of the air hose far enough away from the unit to protect the delicate wires and items inside.

After every six rolls of paper that run through your graph, it is

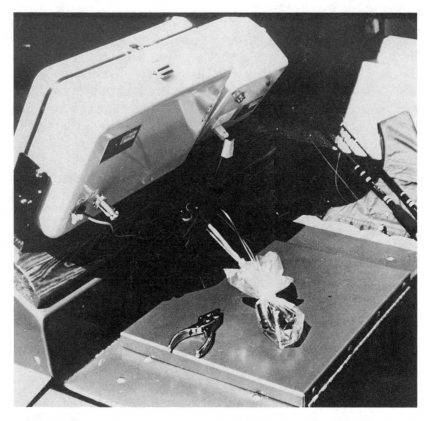

When the boat is not in use, you can use a small plastic sack to protect the power plug and transducer jack from corrosion. Put the sack on after every use.

a good idea to use a clean cloth moistened with alcohol for cleaning off the stylus belt and the belt wheels. *Do not* use solvents which are stronger than the alcohol, and don't use abrasive cleaners for this job. The clear plastic viewing door of the graph and the metal or plastic plate behind the paper should be cleaned often with a soft rag dampened only with clean, fresh water.

Most graph recorders have a rubber or plastic roller which draws or pulls the paper through the unit. This roller will be covered with dust after long use and the dust buildup can cause the paper to slip on the roller and move through the unit in an irregular manner. Clean the take-up roller thoroughly with an alcohol-saturated cotton swab.

The stylus belt on many graphs will stretch with use. This creates poor image reproduction on the paper and/or gaps and blank spaces. When the belt stretches, centrifugal force pushes the stylus out and away from the paper, so there are no readings on the paper during this period. This usually occurs at readings between 20 and 30 feet on a 60-foot scale, or in the upper one-third area of the paper. Replace the stylus belt when this happens. If you're on the water and don't have a spare belt in the boat, try bending the stylus slightly toward the paper. That should help until you can get a replacement belt.

Miscellaneous Chores

The unit's mounting bracket should be checked frequently. Even though the bracket may be secured to the console with large bolts (as suggested earlier), it can become loose from constant pounding and vibration. When your depthfinder shakes and rat-

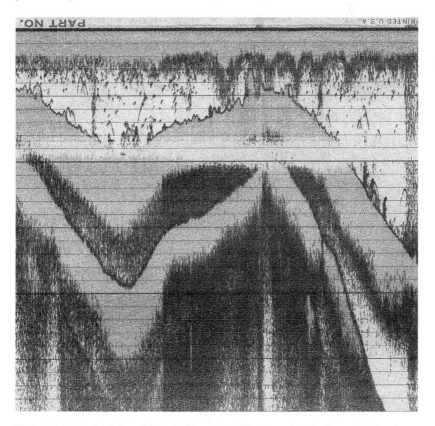

With use, some stylus belts will stretch. This causes a blank space on the chart paper (as shown here), which is usually in the upper third portion of the paper.

tles, it will have a shorter life. Tighten the mounting bracket bolts so the brackets remain secure at all times.

Depthfinders should be removed before the boat is trailered. This eliminates unnecessary vibrations, and is an obvious deterrent to theft, as well.

After use in saltwater, your depthfinder should be wiped off carefully. A cloth dampened with fresh water should do the trick. Just run the wet cloth over the exterior of the unit, not inside. *Do not* dunk the depthfinder in the bathtub to remove salt spray!

Don't attempt to lubricate the moving parts of your depthfinder unless the owner's manual gives exact instructions on how to do it. Even then, use less lubricant than you think is needed, and keep your hands away from the circuits.

Once or twice a season, check out the power and transducer cords in the boat for evidence of rubbing or chafing. Sometimes they wander from their original location, finding sharp edges in the boat to make friends with. You may have to tape these wires up and out of the way again.

Unless your depthfinder is specifically designated as being waterproof, it makes good sense to protect it from moisture to the extent practical. Letting the depthfinder get totally soaked in a downpour does little to improve sonar relations. If the manufacturer provides a rain cover for the unit, use it. A large plastic bag will do the job, too. Protect your depthfinder just as you would any other expensive piece of electronic gear. And, if the unit does get wet in a rainstorm, let it dry out completely before storing it in a confined space.

Finale

By its very nature, the subject of depthfinders is a very complex one. Previously, it was mentioned that you should clean away the salt residue from the outside case of your unit immediately after returning home. There is another little problem if you use a transom-mounted transducer on an aluminum boat. It's called electrolysis.

Electrolysis occurs in both fresh- and saltwater situations, but is much more common in saltwater because it is a better conductor of electrical current.

For saltwater use, do not buy a bronze transducer to be attached to an aluminum boat. Most manufacturers offer plastic

Even though your sonar unit may be considered weatherproof, it's a good idea to protect the unit from rain when on the lake. A clear plastic bag works well.

transducers—use one. Electrolysis occurs where two dissimilar metals touch, particularly bronze and aluminum. The bronze seems to survive the encounter unscathed, but the aluminum will be eaten away. Plastic transducers foil the chemical reaction which causes electrolysis.

When bronze transducer cases are allowed to become grounded to the battery, as in the case of some older models or by accident, the results are alarmingly spectacular. On wood or fiberglass boats, current flow from the motor block to the transducer will eat up the transducer in only a matter of hours, and the motor can be severely damaged.

Most boats and all major-brand depthfinders have a negative-ground system. If your boat has a positive-ground system, you must use a plastic transducer. It doesn't matter whether the rig is

In saltwater fishing situations, low-frequency sonar units perform the best. In deep water, the bottom contour and big fish are represented more accurately using lower frequencies. This is because high frequency signals are absorbed more by particles in the water.

used in fresh- or saltwater. If in doubt, ask your marine dealer to check it out for you.

Differences in the way sound travels through saltwater have little significance in the way your unit will perform if taken to the ocean on vacation. However, there is a material change in reading the very deep signals if you are using a high-frequency unit designed mainly for freshwater use.

High-frequency units in the 200 kHz range are designed to offer superior resolution between objects; however, those high-frequency mechanics are absorbed more by particles in the water. Depthfinders specifically designed for use in saltwater often have lower frequencies. These show the bottom accurately, and display large fish for you. But, you can forget all the fancy footwork described earlier about "fine points" in interpretation. Saltwater units with 1,000-foot depth scales sometimes have frequencies in the 50 kHz range. Those big boomers probably can shoot signals through the pollution in Biscayne Bay!

Let's Go Fishing!

=10=

Big Bass, Little Bass

Arriving in Houston on the heels of a horrendous thunderstorm, Jack Savage watched marble-sized raindrops pounding the runway. Local residents were smiling and saying, "Isn't it wonderful! We haven't had a good rain like this in months!" Jack paid little attention as he headed for the baggage claim area where he claimed his totally soaked canvas bags and found a cab.

As the cabby chattered and the meter ticked along in unison, Jack began to notice the color of the sky as they drove toward his hotel in Conroe. Thick, grayish-black clouds were massed in a solid wall-to-wall blanket overhead. The rain continued for approximately three days.

Before his arrival, the fish in Lake Conroe had been attacking anything reasonably tied onto monofilament. Jack was working on a writing assignment from a major fishing magazine, documenting fun with professional fisherman Rick Clunn. A very likable and talented chap, Clunn has won all sorts of national titles in competitive fishing circles. He gave Jack a dandy interview on tape as they sat by a window watching it rain. But, even Clunn couldn't make the wet go away.

Another professional fisherman, Randy Fite, also was scheduled to take Jack fishing on Conroe. Fite was alleged to be something of a whiz with depthfinders, and he had promised to share some of his expertise. Another excellent interview was recorded, as rain pounded on the roof.

Professional angler Randy Fite used his sonar knowledge to take this nice bass. After studying the sonar screen, he knows whether or not the bass will bite before he even puts a hook down.

Big Bass, Little Bass

A few days later and only hours before the hotel bill became totally ridiculous, the rain stopped. Randy and Jack dashed to the lake, jumped into Fite's boat and roared off to one of the locals' favorite fishing holes. Jack held on as they zipped across the lake, covering his camera equipment with a jacket to protect it from the soggy air.

Most experienced fishermen know what happens when several tons of water fall into a lake after a long dry spell: Old shorelines are replaced with new ones. Productive structure suddenly goes too deep. Water temperatures change dramatically, and the water gets muddy—it always gets muddy.

"We're gonna have to hunt for them, Jack," Randy said after checking what had been one of his best hotspots only days earlier.

And, hunt they did. Fite circled the structure, motored farther out over some drop-offs and made a pass or two over a deep cut in the bottom, all the while concentrating on his depthfinder. Within minutes, Fite located a school of bass. Jack was impressed. He reached for his rod anxious to get started. But, he was surprised when Fite shook his head, no.

"Those aren't active bass," Randy said casually. "They would be pretty tough to catch. Let's find another bunch." He then pushed the throttle forward as Jack stared in disbelief.

They ran a few miles farther up the lake and again began searching structure with the depthfinder. The graph once again displayed little arches, and Randy smiled. To Jack, the arches looked exactly the same as the earlier ones. But, they looked different to the expert. Turning off the big engine and dropping the trolling motor into position, Randy positioned the boat for casting. They began catching bass almost instantly. When the action slowed, he cranked up again. Then, they went searching for a new school again.

To the uninitiated, what followed was a mind-bending experience. Every time Fite found bass on his graph and said they were "active," the anglers caught fish almost effortlessly, even in spite of the muddy water.

Jack decided to stay one more day and learn the secret to Fite's success (if possible). The following morning they traveled out on the lake to the same areas as before. This time, however, when Randy pronounced a school of bass as "inactive and hard to catch," Jack challenged him. The results—or lack thereof—

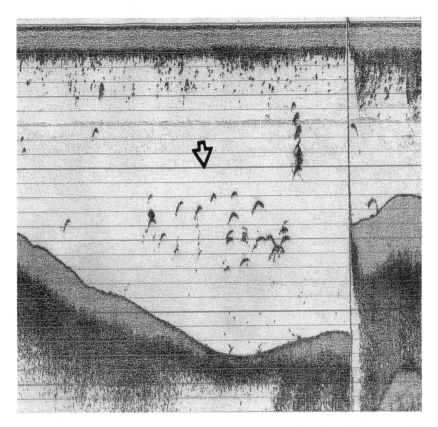

Bass that school loosely (like this) and suspend away from structure are classified as "inactive." If this is the case, move on to more productive areas, but check back every so often.

staunchly supported Fite's expertise in sonar interpretation.

Each time a school of bass appeared on the screen, Randy indicated whether or not they were "active," and politely asked if Jack would like to fish for them. Exhaustive casting to five schools of "inactive" bass produced a total of two fish. The first "active" school yielded nine strikes and seven bass in the boat. The average catch in fishing all active schools was six fish. Until then, Jack (like most anglers) would never have believed you could merely look at a bass school on a paper graph and accurately tell whether the fish would bite or not. Here is Fite's secret: There is a definite pattern to the way bass behave when they are feeding (active) and when they are suspended (inactive). The differences between the two types of behavior are easily detected on a good graph. Because they act in a predictable way, you can use your image burner to

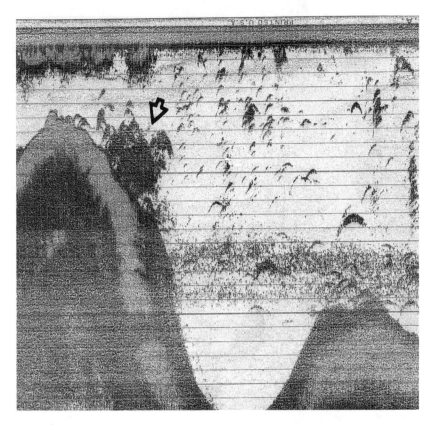

This is what sonar experts are looking for when going after bass. When the fish are tightly schooled and in physical contact with structure, they are actively feeding and highly catchable.

catch more of them. Your ability to *see* them down there will do wonderful things for weighing down your stringer.

When a bass begins to feed, it approaches structure in the water that is holding forage. A bass will actually make physical contact with the structure in order to gobble minnows and crayfish that live there. When the bass is full and wants nothing more than to relax, daydream or rest peacefully, it pulls a short distance away from the structure and suspends. It's reasonable to assume you will catch more bass when they are hungry and feeding than when they're stationary with full stomachs. How the bass relates physically to the structure tells you when you have your best chance to fill your limit.

You can see when bass come into contact with structure by watching where the arches appear on the paper. When the fish signals on your graph are several feet away from the structure, the fish are going to be uncooperative at best. Your best bet is to move to another part of the lake in hopes that other schools are on a different schedule. It is wise to continue checking from time to time on the inactive school—they need to eat sooner or later.

Another reason why feeding bass appear on your graph a certain way is because they school. Inactive bass avoid conversation with others. But, as bass begin to feed, they bunch more tightly together. This is probably a bit of the old killer instinct in them. A wolf pack in the north woods bands together and uses teamwork to down a much larger prey. Bass probably have some of that same predator ingenuity when chasing things they like to eat.

With a graph, you can observe how bass relate to structure, and you can tell if they are going to bite readily or not. It's true. Interestingly enough, when deep-water conditions get lousy, and the bass have to live several feet above the structure, it still works. They suspend off to one side above the structure, but when they begin feeding, they move directly over it.

Most children begin their adventures in bass fishing by using live shiners under big cork floats. While shiner fishing is certainly a highly productive method for catching bass, it typically is restricted to shallow-water areas during specific times of the year. At other times, bass prefer to hang out in deeper water. When bass move into deeper water, depthfinders really earn their keep.

The average bass fisherman seems to define "deep water" for his pursuits as anything over 10 or 11 feet. Working shallow water in the spring and fall can be quite productive. An angler may follow the shoreline tossing various lures at shallow structure, and score. But, in winter and summer, fish seem to prefer deeper haunts. It is at these times that sonar gear will be effective.

While anglers may have little luck at catching bass below the 25-foot mark, they take a respectable number at depths close to that around an underwater island which may be surrounded by *really* deep water. Your success in finding these islands or "humps" in the lake is achieved with sonar use. And, while it is true that bass normally are found in more shallow waters in spring and fall, you also can motor out to where an old creek bed enters the lake and find excellent action in deeper water.

The point is, don't let your idea of bass fishing revolve around shallow water only, regardless of how you define what is "shallow

Rick Clunn is another top professional who relies heavily upon depthfinders for fishing success. Sonar units help achieve the consistency level required in professional fishing.

or deep." Your sonar equipment has limited use in the real shallows because it can only cover a very small portion of the bottom at close range.

If you haven't experienced the fun of catching bass that are suspended over deep structure in winter or summer, you have missed a lot of action!

Fall is a good time for bass fishing. You can find bass in both shallow and deep water, and as a bonus, the larger bass are becoming active again after a long, lazy summer. At this time of year, accurate use of depthfinders can produce spectacular success, allowing you to concentrate your work in productive water.

Regarding shallow-water efforts, creek channels are prime places to fish. You might begin working the creek mouth, where water is about 10 to 12 feet deep on the channel's shoulder, then continue working as it tapers down to perhaps 20 to 25 feet in the channel itself. Using your sonar to stay on course, begin working the channel banks systematically as you progress along the creek. Bass don't always hold right on the lip of the channel, but they stay pretty close.

A lead spoon is quite effective for working a creek channel. It gets to the bottom quickly and is easy to cast. Bounce it on the lip and let it fall into the channel. Make the lure "hop" a couple of times, then repeat the procedure. You can use the depthfinder while "criss-crossing" the channel with the boat to find structure and stay in the productive area.

Creeks filled with brush might best be worked with shallow-running crankbaits. Run the lure deep enough to clear the top of the brush. (You are trying to locate the fish at this point, not fill the ice chest, so use a lure that can be worked efficiently on the structure.) When you find the fish, switch to more "deliberate" techniques which may work better.

As you move farther up into the creek, switch to a smaller size crankbait, worm or jig. Usually, bass found back in the creek during the fall will be smaller than those still out near the main lake in deeper water. If there have been several below-freezing nights, as sometimes happens in fall, you may have to switch to a *very* tiny bait. Fast-dropping water temperatures will clobber those fish in shallow places. Their metabolism will slow down to an approximate state of shock, and it will take tiny baits worked *very* slowly to get them.

Another good spot for finding fall bass is a moss bed. Bass love moss beds, and the action can be excellent at almost any time of day. Here again, use the lure that seems best suited for an initial encounter with bass. Crankbaits would likely be fouled most of the time; so would spoons. Spinnerbaits would be an ideal choice for use in searching for bass around moss beds. The plastic worm would work well, also, but it might be too slow if you have a larger area to cover.

Cover the moss bed completely. Work the lure all around the outside edges, over the top and in the middle where there are pockets. Bass could be holding practically anywhere in the structure. They could be just sitting off to one side admiring it.

Rock and riprap, identified on your graph, will hold a surprising number of bass in the fall months, too. The best method for fishing that type of structure is to position your boat near the edge and cast up or down the shoreline, bringing the lure back parallel to it. Crankbaits or spinnerbaits worked from 1 to 5 feet away from the edge produce well.

One expert breaks down fall fishing into two parts: "early fall" and "late fall." This is because of changes in the oxygen levels you may find in so many lakes at this time of year. For example, September may be considered part of summer in some areas, and the lake may have bad oxygen in the deep-water areas. This pushes more fish into the shallow-water areas, obviously. In November, the oxygen is usually good down to the 18- to 25-foot range. Many bass will move back out in the lake to deeper structure, depending on water temperature.

You can pattern your fishing around a number of things, but one of the most important is what is displayed on the depthfinder.

An alternative for bass fishing in the fall is deep water, generally interpreted as between 15 and 30 feet. In this situation, the distinction between early and late season is even more critical. Oxygen levels can still be low in most warm-climate areas, causing fish that are out in the main lake to suspend over structure instead of on it. Suspended bass are usually more difficult to catch, and the vertical jigging technique, which often works best, is tough to master.

The plus side of deep-water fall fishing comes from your ability to use your depthfinder to accurately cover a large area of water without ever wetting a line. You don't even have to stop your

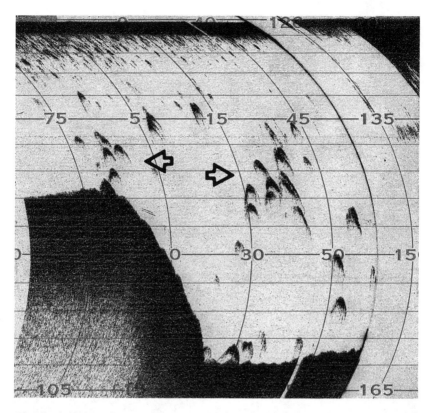

The schooled bass on this curve-line graph are either starting or ending a feeding spree. The fish at right are loosely schooled and away from the structure, while the ones at left are more tightly grouped and in contact with structure.

boat's engine until after you have found fish. The procedure is simply moving from one deep-water structure to the next, checking each spot for fish. If they are on the structure, you can see them with sonar. If not, you merely move on to the next place as there is no point fishing unproductive water. Once you have learned to read your depthfinder well, you can cover a sizable chunk of the lake without wasting time. Also, it helps to have a flasher and a graph in the boat. Locate the structure with the flasher; then check out the action with your graph. Once you have the skills to find active bass before stopping the boat's big engine, your fishing success in deep water will improve fantastically!

Ideally, you might want to have a third depthfinder in the boat. This one would be situated in the bow, with the transducer mounted on the trolling motor. Once active bass have been lo-

Bass professional Don Iorino from Burbank, California, uses a paper graph on the console and an LCG on the casting deck when deep-water jigging on Lake Casitas. Casitas is known for producing some of the world's largest largemouth bass.

cated, the trolling motor sonar unit allows you to stay directly on top of the fish. Successful vertical jigging requires accurate lure presentation.

Your depthfinder cannot tell the difference between a 15-inch bass and a 15-inch carp. It displays either of them the same way on the depthfinder's face, so it's your job to differentiate between bass and other species. In the case of a single fish of moderate size, you need to use your knowledge of fish habitat to "guess" what fish species it is. (A single fish out in deep water away from structure will probably not be a bass.)

Vertical fishing with a spoon, grub or plastic worm is quite effective. You must place the offering accurately in the productive zone, and the difference can be only a matter of a yard or so in cold weather. If fish show up on your unit at a depth of 20 feet, working your bait several feet above or below the school won't do much for your reputation as an expert. And, many times, deep-water bass group together tightly, making it possible for the angler in the bow of the boat to get action with almost every drop, while the angler in the back never gets a hit!

Most strikes (maybe 90 percent) while vertical jigging will come as the lure drops or flutters downward. You can't afford to have slack in your line at that critical moment. So, after you "hop" or pull the lure upward, catch it with your line. Then, follow the lure back down by lowering your rod, keeping the line tight. If you establish a set rhythm for doing this, you'll instantly notice any variation in the way the line acts. Even if you don't feel fish strike, a twitch or slight pause in the line tells you a fish has hit; set the hook immediately.

Deep-water bass fishing is both fun and productive, although most anglers never take it seriously. Learn to use your depthfinders and you'll discover that this method for taking bass is "deadly."

=11=

Crappies

Statistics generated by game and fish agencies in many states put the crappie as No. 1 in popularity among fishermen, even though the majority of anglers consider the species to be active only during a couple of months each year. In truth, crappies make definite, seasonal migrations in the lake, and their movements are quite predictable. Knowing how to use sonar for finding the appropriate structure allows you to catch these fish year-round rather easily.

Most crappie enthusiasts limit their efforts to working shallow structure near shore during the spawning season, usually during March and April. Going offshore to find the fish with a depthfinder never really enters their minds. Basically, the average crappie fisherman believes this species comes in close to the bank during springtime to attack live minnows swimming beneath a cork float, then mysteriously disappears into the great unknown in May.

As technology improved and depthfinders became more sophisticated, a great deal more has been learned about the crappie's seasonal migrations. Serious crappie fishermen can use sonar to follow the fish as they relocate in reaction to water temperature changes. The movements on your favorite lake can be plotted, and the fish there will shift from one type of structure to another annually on a nearly identical schedule. These crappie migrations in large lakes and reservoirs may change slightly from one section of the country to another because their timetables are keyed to

Many crappie fishing experts believe that larger crappies typically spawn in deeper water. Using sonar can be a big advantage when trying to locate these popular fish during this time period.

Crappies

Depthfinders are invaluable for taking crappies during the early, colder months when they move to potential spawning areas. Sonar helps you locate those ridges next to deep water where crappies congregate.

water temperatures. The following pattern shows how these fish move in Tennessee and Kentucky. (You may have to make an adjustment of a month or so to fit the migrations in your area.)

In the really cold months, like January and February, crappies are usually found near deep water around major entrances to large coves in the lake. They require little food and do not feed actively because their metabolism has slowed greatly.

Near the end of February and the first part of March, crappies begin their migration toward shore. Leaving deeper water, they head into the mouths of creeks. The first place they stop is on the mouths' high ridges. They congregate there, and are rather plentiful when you find them. "Hotspots" for action frequently are on these ridges, adjacent to deep water. On warmer days you can enjoy excellent fishing there.

Crappies stay on those high ridges near the mouths of creeks for many days, sometimes for weeks. Early March fishing requires a light touch to detect the faint bite typical in cold water. The fish often merely suck the minnow into the mouth and hold it there. You may even have to raise your pole from time to time to see if you have a fish. (If your friends thought your home movies were boring when they featured your two kids and your funny bird dog, don't waste film on this type of crappie fishing action.) Cold-water crappie fillets do taste better, though. The meat is firmer. And, you usually have the lake to yourself.

In April, crappies begin leaving the ridges, looking for a handy spot for their brief love affairs. They move in closer to shore, scattering everywhere in search of some sort of wooden structure: tree-tops, stumps or brush. Typically, if you find brush piles in reasonably shallow water during April, you will find crappies. They seem to have quite an appetite now, so you normally will have no trouble catching them with minnows or jigs.

Immediately after the spawning season, it is tough trying to find crappies. You will find a number of fish at a particular spot one morning, but after going back to the dock for a sandwich and more minnows, you'll return only to discover the crappies are gone. They just wander around aimlessly for a month or more after spawning. You are forced to search for them with your depth-finder. When you locate a school, however, they bite eagerly.

As the water continues to warm, crappies begin a full-scale migration into the main body of the lake. Not all crappies migrate into the main lake. Some of the smaller ones remain near shore, but, most of them will be gone. By July, they will have established residence along an old riverbed.

Even when the summer sun is hot enough to make your tennis shoes smell like catfish bait, crappies are still the easiest to find and catch regularly. Summertime crappies will definitely gather on an old river channel in most large lakes, and if you exercise a bit of patience, you can fill your stringer. First, find the shoulder of the channel with your depthfinder, then find some structure associated with it. Their depth can vary, but they usually will be found between 15 and 25 feet down on the slope into the channel. Because it's a river channel, you may have several *miles* of productive area to explore and enjoy. And, as a bonus, you'll find several other species sharing the same accommodations. Challenge after challenge awaits you.

The fish pack up in September and migrate again. September and October are both *excellent* months for crappie fishing fun. They're back in the creek mouths, having returned to approximately the same places they were at in March (the high spots on ridges). They do not school as tightly now, but they stay put rather than wandering again. When you find them on your sonar, you'll have plenty of fun in store.

As the weather continues to cool down in October, the fish take a step backward; they return to the entrances of big coves and bays. Again, they take to the high ground immediately next door to deep water. And, they make up their minds to stay there until the waters get warmer. Crappies will stay in these areas throughout the winter. Then, in late February or early March, they move again, heading for the good times along the shoreline.

Very few species of fish lend themselves to depthfinder location better than crappies do. Their movements and migrations are predictable with a good degree of accuracy. Sonar skills help you find their little wet noses with ease.

It is evident that crappies move into the shore to spawn during the early spring, but the activity is not one which can be pegged to an exact calendar date. Many anglers have been planning vacations months in advance to coincide with the crappie spawning runs, only to discover the action was much better the week before—or the week after.

During the spring, crappies can be rather unpredictable. This is due in part to the things which affect their daily life. Spring itself is unpredictable in nature. When the weather breaks and there are several gorgeous, warm days in a row, the females move into shallow water, preparing to lay their eggs. Then, it rains, or turns cold and the temperature drops. The females react by retreating into deeper water, playing a "wait-and-see" game.

In bodies of water which eventually flow through a man-made dam, spawning crappies are often influenced by the person who controls the gates. They may move into shallower water, find a housesite, and awake the next morning to find the gatekeeper has dropped the lake level several inches. Heavy spring rains often make gatekeepers do things like that. Again, the crappie must back off to reconsider.

Combinations and changes in water level and temperature make it practically impossible to pick the exact date and location for crappies to spawn. The spawning season usually will cover a four-to-six week period, with fish coming and going steadily like picnic ants hot on the trail of a honey bun. There can be little doubt of finding crappies near shore in springtime, but exactly *where* they are on a given day is not all that easy to determine.

The Crappie's Seasonal Migrations

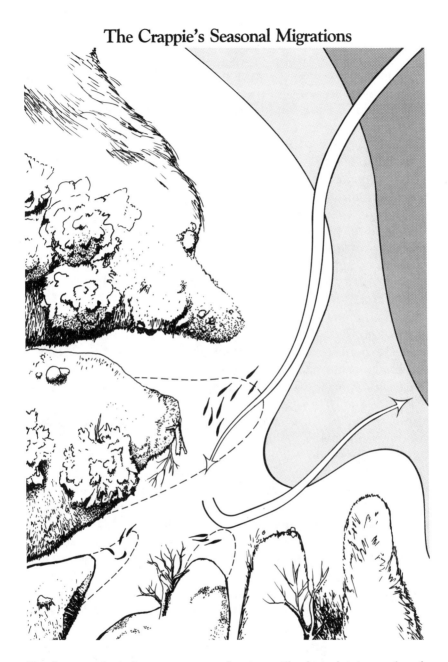

This illustration depicts how crappies seasonally migrate. They begin their journey from the deeper waters in early spring (top right-hand corner) and move into shallower waters (follow the arrow). They head for creek mouths, congregating at ridges. Then, it's time for spawning. They move in closer to shore and structure. As waters warm, and summer begins, they migrate back to the main lake.

They can be almost anywhere in the general area of the creek mouths—shallow, deep and suspended.

Depthfinders help fishermen find the underwater structure that crappies like: drop-offs, creek channels, stickups and stumps. While bank fishing for spawning crappies is the most popular technique, backing your boat out into the open water over structure can produce consistent results as well. For one thing, all crappies do not go to the shallows for spawning at the same time. This is why the activity lasts for several weeks. New arrivals move in all the time. And, they cruise the offshore structure *both* coming to and going from the shore. Bank fishing may be unpredictable because of weather conditions, but catching crappies several yards away from shore on structure is a sure bet.

Many crappie experts are convinced the really large crappies spawn in 8- to 12-foot water, around stumps. Another reason to work water away from the bank.

An efficient tackle and technique for catching deeper-water crappies consists of two hooks spaced about 18 inches apart, with a 1- or 2-ounce lead weight attached to the line either between the hooks or an additional 18 inches below the bottom hook. With a lively minnow on each hook, the procedure is to "walk" or "bounce" the lead weight along the structure surface. You actually can "feel" the lead weight touching the structure if you concentrate on keeping the line tight.

With the two hooks separated in this manner, you are offering the bait at different levels simultaneously. Generally, you'll find most fish will hit either one or the other. That small difference in depth can make a big difference. Of course, you can catch two crappies at the same time on occasion. Thin wire hooks are used because this procedure often results in snags on the structure. With practice, you learn to raise and lower your pole gently when the rig gets hung up. Usually, the lead weight will dislodge the tangled hook on its way downward. If this fails, pulling straight up on the line will straighten the thin hooks so they will release from the structure.

Sensitive poles, usually between 10 and 15 feet in length, work best for use with the bottom-bumping method. You can buy a fiberglass pole with the needed sensitivity, use a cane pole that has a good, flexible tip, or convert your old fly rod into a crappie-catching tool. It helps to have a line-keeper on the pole. You can

After you've located deep-water crappies with sonar, double-hook rigs are extremely effective. Occasionally, you can catch two crappies at the same time. This helps fill your stringer fast.

Crappies

Depthfinders help anglers locate structure that attract crappies. If your unit indicates a drop-off, creek channel or stump, chances are good you'll find a nice crappie like this nearby.

wrap excess line around the spool or cleat and use it later when you enter deeper water where additional monofilament is needed to reach bottom.

Tight-line fishing, or "bottom bumping," is fantastically productive on crappies every month of the year. When you feel a fish tap the bait, set the hook immediately; don't wait for it to tote the lead weight off somewhere. You should use at least 15-pound monofilament line for this technique. You'll need enough line strength to straighten out the wire hooks which refuse to "jiggle" free of brush. And, you may need it for landing a much larger fish that might take your minnow down there. Tales of boating big bass and catfish on these crappie rigs are common.

Some professional crappie guides use 40-pound test line for their double-hook rigs. They don't want to waste time on snags, or spend the day tying on new terminal tackle for their customers. If the water you fish is somewhat murky, you probably can use the heavy stuff. But, if your lake is fairly clear, you'll catch more fish by using line in the 15- to 20-pound class.

12

Stripers

When a big striper takes your bait, he is about as subtle as a trainwreck. One second you're sitting there holding the rod casually, and the next second you're trying desperately to hang onto it! Gears in the reel's drag mechanism are whizzing noisily, line is disappearing rapidly from the spool and your rod is being pulled powerfully downward. All this happens, of course, only if the fish failed in his initial attempt to jerk the entire rod and reel out of your hands and take it with him into the water. The sensation is not unlike having your hook snagged unexpectedly by a nuclear sub passing below at full speed.

Professional striper guides get a special kick out of taking people fishing who have never experienced the raw power of a heavy striper's strike or the battle which follows. Universally, the uninitiated will utter some kind of whoop or war cry in astonishment, the sound usually emanating from deep in the gut. Occasionally, the screaming will continue nonstop during the ensuing battle until the client has lost his voice. For the remainder of the day, then, the guide and client will most likely have to communicate with hand signals.

Guide and outdoor writer Mark Williams recalls his first experience with stripers in the mid-'70s, fishing with a pal on Percy Priest Lake near Nashville, Tennessee:

"My initiation to freshwater fury came shortly after I discovered how hard it is to breathe while clawing the gunwale to hold

Nice stripers like this are the reward for diligent work with depthfinders. Stripers are easily recognized on the screen. Be prepared for lots of action when you find them.

Stripers

on in a bass boat doing 60 mph across a frigid lake in March.

"Percy Priest had been stocked with striper fingerlings in 1968, and the fish had grown dramatically in size during the years afterward. I had heard stories about striper fishing, but had been entirely too busy writing magazine copy and romancing a new bride to tax my heart further with anything new.

"I was talked into an early spring striper trip by a local chap who had been enjoying spectacular action on the lake for years. We met at the dock, backed the boat into partially-thawed water, and headed out into the lake. Bill had not revealed in prior conversations that he had suicidal tendencies—a fact which became extremely evident moments after we cleared the 'no wake' buoys at the marina.

"The huge engine catapulted his small, lightweight bass boat across the lake with breathtaking, eye-watering speed as I frantically tried to hold on in what must have been an instant-500 chill factor. My Barbour coat broke the cold on my arms and chest, but my face and hands burned like crazy.

"After finally depriving the monster motor of fuel and allowing it to grumble reluctantly at idle for a few minutes before shutting it off, Bill positioned the boat with his trolling motor. We began casting topwater redfins and wobbling them back across underwater humps and along shoreline ledges. This produced only a couple of half-hearted swirls a foot or so behind the lure. My mentor then declared we should troll for a while. This we did, using a deep-running Hellbender to which was tied a large white doll fly on 3 feet of 30-pound monofilament as a trailer. A chunk of pork rind was attached to the leadhead and I winced as the big engine roared to life again. Bill apparently does everything fast, including trolling.

"The short, stubby trolling rod Bill gave me to use was bending the bones in my left forearm as it strained against the drag created by the big lure throbbing 75 feet behind the boat. Then, suddenly, something grabbed the plug, causing the rod to lurch violently out over the transom, taking my white knuckles with it. When both my arms were extended fully as I maintained a death grip on the rod, something went 'pop' between my shoulder blades, and the fight was on.

"The 21-pound striper ripped and ran for what seemed like an hour, but was probably more like a half-minute per pound. When the fish finally gave up only moments before I did, Bill used his over-sized net to bring it over the side, then collapsed in a fit of laughter, trying to describe my antics while fighting the big fish.

"We congratulated each other, he turned the boat around for another pass down the channel, and we did it all over again. The morning ended with four big stripers standing on their heads in the small livewell like flowers in a vase. We had our Tennessee limit of stripers, and I was hooked on the fun for life."

Mark eventually became one of the better striper guides in the Southeast after relocating in the Carolinas with his family. His account of getting "hooked" on striper fishing action is not unlike the way most other anglers react after experiencing the sheer fun and excitement these heavy-duty brawlers can provide.

Sonar expertise plays a huge part in striper fishing success. This species roams a lake almost constantly. And, documented studies show that certain fish, sporting little radio transmitters, have traveled over 20 miles throughout a lake in only a matter of days! On the other hand, stripers have been found on or near the same structure for many days in succession. It may have been a seasonal change in their travel plans, or maybe the structure was so appealing that a new school moved in every time an old one left. Stripers are very structure-oriented just like other gamefish, even though they often cruise a lake's big, open-water areas.

Stripers also have a habit of intimidating schools of shad, literally "herding" them into a cove or pocket somewhere, then chopping them up viciously during a feeding spree. At these times, structure may not enter the picture in relation to what is *beneath* the fish, but water depth and the ability to confine their prey becomes important. When feeding stripers chase baitfish into a shallow part of the lake, you can see the surface action from quite a distance. And, when you find yourself in the middle of a feeding school like that, it sounds as if someone is throwing concrete blocks into the water. The first time you experience this, you may fear for the safety of small children in the boat.

You can tie on almost any old lure you like and feed it to the fish, as long as the action stays frantic. Topwater enthusiasts go absolutely bananas over this sort of thing.

Finding a ravenous school of stripers in the process of reducing the shad population in shallow water is indeed fun. But, it happens only rarely to the fisherman who has to work for a living.

Finding a school of ravenous stripers feeding in shallow water is the topwater specialist's dream. It's the kind of excitement not every angler experiences.

Most fish probably will be taken from April to September with live bait. You find the school with your sonar, use the trolling motor to position the boat over them, and fish straight down. In warm weather, the fish may be cruising about 15 to 20 feet below the surface. In hot weather, they often go much deeper.

Where legal, live bream are very popular as a spring and summer striper fishing bait. Shiners and goldfish work well, too. And, below many dams, you can use a long-handled net to scoop shad for bait, as they often swim in huge schools along the bank when power is being generated. If a striper is even slightly hungry, it will smack a shad that's presented on its nose. Bream are probably the next best choice for bait.

After you've used your depthfinder to locate the stripers, place your bait at exactly the depth where they are, keeping it there with the help of a lead sinker positioned 1 or 2 feet above the hook. If school fish signals are showing up at 20 feet on the screen, you want that bait to be exactly 20 feet under the transducer. Many live-bait striper fishermen wrap colored thread around their fishing rods 12 inches out from the reel face. Using the 12-inch mark, they strip out line by hand, counting the feet until the bait

Your best choice for bait when fishing for stripers is shad. Because shad group together in huge schools below dams, anglers can predictably fill their bait buckets for a successful day of fishing.

Stripers

is at the desired depth. It works beautifully!

With a good depthfinder, and very little wind or current tugging at your line, you can *watch* your bait go down through the transducer's cone. You don't have to strip out the line in increments for accuracy; let the bait fall as you concentrate on the depthfinder. When it reaches the fish, you just stop the line flow by engaging the reel. Obviously, if you don't drop the bait down through the cone, you can't watch it fall.

Fishing with live bait becomes something of a chore if the fish are not hungry. You can stay on top of them half the day and never get a strike. Fortunately, those situations usually are rare. Even if the school is not taking offers, usually a few mean and aggressive characters will whack your bait just for the sake of killing it.

Live-bait fishing also offers the best shot at taking stripers on ultra-light tackle. The idea may sound strange, knowing how these fish behave when hooked. But, if your depthfinder shows no trees or other brush below when stripers are found, you might pull it off.

If you really want to test your skills with rod and reel, spool up some light line on a small outfit and take a crack at using it to boat a striper. You must be sure there are no underwater structures nearby that can cause problems for the light line. Examine the bottom carefully by increasing the sensitivity on your depthfinder a bit. Placing a sharp hook into a striper's mouth seems to give the fish an almost uncontrollable urge to tie monofilament in knots around tree branches.

Vertical jigging for stripers can produce excellent tablefare, too. Almost any of the rectangular metal jigs or lead spoons will work quite well, provided they are heavy enough to be worked effectively. A chunk of pork rind sometimes gives the lure more appeal. Other lures, like leadheads with plastic tails, will produce effectively, also.

Over the years, co-author Buck Taylor has become a top striper expert. His specialty is taking huge stripers on ultra-light tackle; he can boast of numerous trophy catches on 4-, 6- and 8-pound line. He has established, and then broken, his personal line-class records on several Tennessee lakes over the years.

Fishing a favorite spot one October morning on Norris Lake in east Tennessee, Buck found a few stripers holding quite deep. He tried enticing them with a 5-inch Sassy Shad. The lure is heavy,

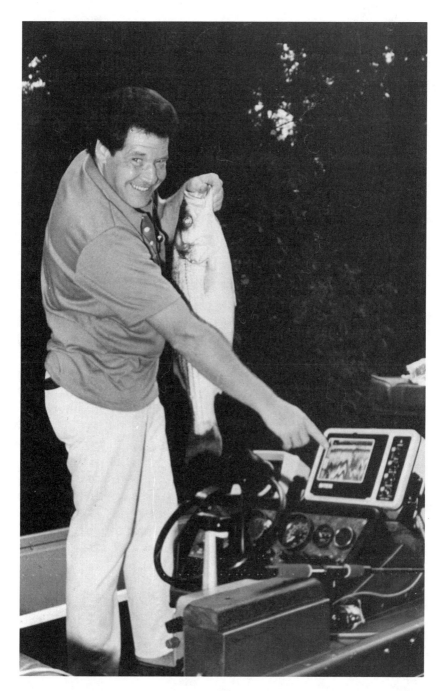

When the depthfinder shows that there are no underwater trees, you can use ultra-light tackle to take stripers; there are no branches for the striper to wrap the light line around.

Stripers

has a soft, flexible tail and is well-suited for deep jigging. There was no action until he decided to leave.

The stripers that Buck had spotted on his depthfinder were holding right on bottom in 52 feet of water. He could tell by the signal size on the screen that these were large fish; however, they still weren't taking the bait after 15 minutes of working the pearl-and-blue jig under their noses. Deciding to try another spot, Buck began bringing up his lure. A couple of cranks on the reel and the line stopped coming up; it began going out.

Norris Lake, probably the oldest lake in the Tennessee Valley Authority chain, is clear and deep. (All underwater trees and stump rows have long since gone the way of the dinosaurs, leaving the lake bottom clean and snag-free.) This makes it ideal for the use of ultra-light gear, and Buck had spooled 8-pound monofilament for the trip.

When the fish began swimming off with his lure, Buck set the hook and the fight began. More accurately, the waiting began. It's hard to get a big striper's attention when you cannot exert force with light line. Granted, 8-pound line is barely considered to be in the ultra-light family of monofilament string, but Buck was using a new rod and reel. He had been more concerned with discovering how the new rod cushioned powerful runs and the reel drag system handled stress, than in setting records on that particular morning.

Buck knew almost instantly that the fish was heavy by the way it acted: staying deep and making long, powerful sprints. Using his trolling motor to follow the fish and keep at least *some* line on the reel, Buck was treated to a tour of the area as the big striper made repeated, authoritative runs. After almost 20 minutes of straining the light rod into a horseshoe curve, the fish began to tire as did Buck's arms. Finally, the striper surfaced. It rolled and floundered like a walrus in a feather bed.

Buck eased the boat over toward the fish, keeping his line tight and rod high. After positioning the boat alongside the over-sized striper, Buck grabbed it by the lip, dropped the rod and used both hands to bring the striper aboard. The fish stretched from one side of the boat to the other, its nose touching the rod locker on one side and its tail curled up against the gunwale on the other. Quite a nice fish.

The trophy catch pulled the scales down past the 35-pound

Buck Taylor poses with his world-record striper that was caught on 8-pound monofilament line. Learning to use and interpret sonar pays off in the end—ask Buck!

Stripers 167

Finding stripers with your depthfinder and getting them to blast a jumbo topwater lure is great fun.

mark, easily qualifying it for line-class, world-record status at the time. Buck has caught bigger fish since, and he still sets records. But, that special morning on Norris Lake remains a favorite example for him of the definitive excitement available when personal skill and the use of sonar information are combined.

Topwater excitement, striper style, can be extremely exciting and stressful. Usually, during the first six weeks of spring's warming weather, stripers are prone to boil the water beneath a jumbo-sized lure pulled across the surface. Good equipment and good fishing techniques are essential. (Nerves of steel are recommended.)

In contrast to the occasional times when feeding stripers can be seen ripping shad and splashing water great distances, most topwater excitement will come when the action is far less visible. You may see no indication whatsoever of stripers in the area. The surface may be calm and unbroken. Sometimes, there will be a swirl or two which will betray their presence.

Stripers will rocket up through 10 or more feet of water to nail a topwater lure. You can find them ready and anxious to do this on many mornings, and sometimes even all day if it's overcast. When fish are holding near the bottom, close to islands, near underwater humps and by bends in the channel, they cannot always be spotted on the depthfinder without spooking them with your engine. If they are 15 feet or more down, the boat doesn't seem to bother them quite as much (unless you rev the engine).

Topwater action involving stripers is not a matter usually kept secret by profit-conscious dock operators. Many (not all) of them will point you to within a few hundred yards of where the reported action is happening. If you can get that close, reasonably competent use of sonar will surely locate the shelf, hump or bend they are using that morning. Look for it in water less than 15 feet deep. Long, sloping points can be the ideal spot for searching.

When you find a likely spot, quietly back away to the maximum distance you can cast a big lure. The magnum Redfins and Rebel topwater jobs are generally accepted as the best lures for this. Cast the lure as far over or across the flat as you can, then let it sit a second or two. It's a good idea to take up the slack in your line the instant the lure splashes down. This is because, many times, that's when the fish pops it. The retrieve with these 6- to 9-inch lures should be painfully slow. All you want to do is force the lure to make a "V" wake on the surface as it comes back in. No jerks, no trying to make it pop and gurgle and no darting, stop-start action. Just a slow, deliberate retrieve across the surface. It drives 'em wild!

Topwater striper fishing requires strong line. You should not take a crack at it with line that tests under 12 pounds. And, 15-pound test line is better. Some anglers use 30-pound line, maybe even heavier. However, anything over 20-pound test can cut the distance you can cast the lure.

For reasons known only by the fish, stripers often strike violently at a topwater plug but miss it by as much as a foot. When you have made a long cast and allowed the plug to rest for a moment, start the slow retrieve. Logically, you hope something will happen. Your nervous system is coiled like a compressed steel spring, your heart is beating excitedly and your eyes and ears are straining for any evidence of a strike. When it happens, you react instantly. Without practice, you can't do otherwise.

The trick is to convince your nerves that the awesome explosion in the water at your lure is nothing to worry about. If done properly, the act of setting the hook should be almost in self-defense. When the monster smashes your lure, you *feel* it; when he misses it, you don't feel the fish on the line. Set the hook only when you feel the hit.

Setting the hook on a striper that rips into a surface lure is almost a matter of self-defense. When the fish takes the lure, you will feel it immediately. Set the hook when you feel the hit.

Complete Angler's Library

When a striper misses a topwater plug, you should calmly stop the forward motion of the lure and let it sit there motionless. The word "calmly" is used in jest. But, you *should* stop the lure. After perhaps four or five seconds, begin the slow retrieve again. Often, the fish will attack it a second time.

On days with cloud cover for extended periods, you can catch topwater stripers practically the entire time—if you can stay with them. Occasionally, a heavy morning or afternoon overcast will make the fish come up even in summer, especially if the overcast remains after a fresh, soft rain.

If you're live-bait fishing, vertical jigging or topwater trolling or casting, stripers will give you a "thrill a minute" if not more. They offer some heavy-duty brawls for the angler who can find them on the lake. And, you can do it regularly with what you know about sonar.

=====13=====

Walleyes

What better tablefare is there than a brace of 2-pound walleyes fresh from the water? Nothing definite comes to mind, and that's exactly the reason why these golden-sided beauties are so intently pursued by millions of anglers across the country. Walleyes swim in waters from Canada to Mississippi, and from Maine to Wyoming (thanks to stocking programs). Washington's and Oregon's border river, the Columbia, is also home to trophy marble-eyes.

But, let's not forget the sporting opportunities they offer. They may not have the aerial abilities of a smallmouth or a rainbow, but they are scrappers. They run for the bottom to find shelter, and any fish of more than a few pounds will show you how well your reel's drag is working, especially if it's in an aggressive mood.

That fact was driven home one fall day when two anglers were trolling a large, shallow point on Minnesota's Lake Winnibigoshish. The walleyes were stacked, and feeding; there was no doubt of this, as nearly every boat on the lake was concentrated on one particular point.

They had caught a number of fish on live-bait rigs, but wanted to try a new purple, fire tiger ThunderStick crankbait. Grabbing the nearest of spare rods, a 6-foot baitcaster strung with 12-pound monofilament, one of the anglers tied on and let fly. Two cranks into the retrieve, the lure was hit so hard that he lost his grip on the handle. Luckily, the rig fell inside the boat. Trying not to show embarrassment to the several dozen anglers who witnessed

Few anglers realize the fishing potential of main-lake open water. Keith Kavajecz and partner Gary Parsons have developed their unique trolling technique over a number of years.

Walleyes

the misplay, he retrieved the rod and started cranking.

The fish had other plans, however, and launched a protest that pulled yard after yard of the heavy line off the reel. The other anglers' giggles turned to hushed whispers when they realized what was happening. Both they and he knew that fish was a *big* one.

The walleye was never weighed, though. As the angler placed it into the livewell, he guessed it would barely break 3½ pounds. He had been taken to the mat by a fish that was far from "trophy" status. Worse still, he could hear the beginnings of muted laughter coming from the other boats.

The point of the tale is that walleyes can perform the unexpected. That fish was obviously intent on eating something, and when it discovered it had been fooled, was just as intent on getting away. Never mind that it didn't turn out to be a wall-hanger, the 3-pounder provided the most excitement of the day, even though the angler couldn't enjoy the glory of a well-fought fight with a lunker.

The walleye's uncanny ability to elude anglers is another aspect that attracts fishermen. It's part of the walleye *mystique*. That's what this chapter deals with—location, and how your sonar gear can help you find walleyes. But, it's also important to remember that sonar is not the only factor in pinpointing your quarry. You need a good understanding of where the fish are likely to be on a particular body of water. Are they in the weeds? Will they be on the rocks? How about that breakline?

Use your electronics to locate the spot, and your fishing knowledge to build confidence that you'll find walleyes there. Then, if you see those magic "hooks" near the weeds, rocks or break, you know you're truly open for business.

Early Walleyes

After spawning, walleyes start a general movement toward their summertime haunts. It doesn't happen all at once, and all the walleyes in a body of water won't go to the same place. But, there are certain areas to key on—high-percentage areas that are good places to begin your search. If you don't find fish on a certain type of structure, try another type. It's a game of hide-and-seek until you figure out the pattern. Moreover, because lakes differ in physical makeup, walleyes could be at different stages in the annual cycle. Fishfinders make the task a lot easier.

Three LCGs are used in this angler's boat, giving extreme accuracy when searching for walleyes. One is a side-scanning unit, a second delivers a conventional display and the third is set on a split-screen to show both an LCG flasher dial and a regular bottom reading.

"On large, relatively shallow lakes, you should generally be fishing shallow water during the early part of the season," says Scott Glorvigen, Minnesota walleye guide and veteran of both the Masters Walleye Circuit (MWC) and Professional Walleye Trail (PWT). "Shoreline flats near spawning areas are good places to start."

Glorvigen runs four sonar units on his tiller boat: one Bottom Line 6600 at the back where he can see it from the operator's seat, another on the front casting deck and two Sidefinder Scouts, also at the rear station. Both transducers are mounted on the transom, one pointing right, the other left.

Because the water he fishes during this time of year (on these shallow lakes) is normally less than 8 feet deep, you'd think that sonar gear would be completely useless. Not true! Glorvigen relies on the bottom-pointing units to pinpoint subtle inconsistencies on the bottom that hold walleyes. "I put the LCG into the split-screen mode, with one half showing the water column from top to bottom and the other half tracking the bottom," he says. "It gives you a better idea of what's down there."

What he looks for are subtle changes—patches of last year's weeds (maybe with a bit of new growth), an area where sand turns to gravel, or "anything that's a little different." The grayline feature on his LCG shows him where the bottom composition changes. If you run a flasher, notice how the return signal narrows and dims as you move over a soft bottom, or widens and grows brighter as you move over a hard one.

Once found, live-bait rigs or jig-and-minnow combinations work well on these fish. Because the walleyes could still be lethargic as a result of the rigors of spawning, or the water is cold, start with a slow presentation. Increase the speed until you find just the right action. If you think the fish may be spooked by the boat passing overhead, it's time to break out the side planers. They take your bait far enough away from the commotion to negate its effects. Small, in-line models are inexpensive and work wonders on boat-shy walleyes.

"One thing about this type of fishing is that it can be frustrating at times," he says. "You make these long drifts in 5 to 8 feet of water, picking up a fish here, one over there, then the action stops. You have to figure out where the fish went." Until he discovered the side-scanning sonar, Glorvigen says it was a hit-or-miss proposition. "Now I can scan the deeper water on one side of the boat, and the shallower water on the other. Side-scanners make things a lot simpler."

As mentioned before, walleyes behave differently in various types of lakes. On deeper natural lakes, you may find them on large points or in bays near spawning sites if you can't pin them down on flats.

Then again, remember that walleyes can be unpredictable. During one of the early MWC tournaments, Glorvigen recalls a situation that he describes as a "humbling experience." It involved walleye legends Mike McClelland, Bob Propst, Gary Roach and Randy Amenrud.

"The tournament took place on a northern Minnesota lake," he said. "Most competitors, including my brother Marty and I,

　　　　Complete Angler's Library

Deep Flat On Lake

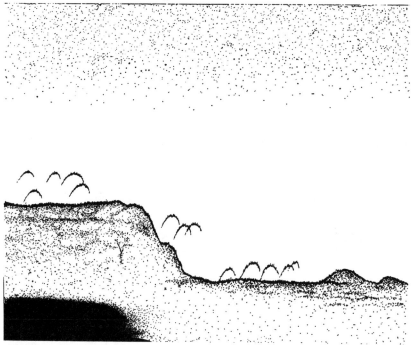

Many walleyes in large lakes use expansive, deep-water flats throughout the summer. If you find them scattered on the flat's top, they'll be aggressive; and, a fast-paced trolling presentation works best. If they're located along the slope where the flat drops into deeper water, their activity level is usually borderline and those at the slope's bottom are normally inactive; therefore, a slow, precise approach, usually jigging, is the best method.

were concentrating on shallower structure. All of a sudden, we noticed McClelland and Propst in one boat and Roach and Amenrud in another, working the bottom of a deep break."

The two teams were obviously not fishing where they were *supposed* to be fishing. And whether the rest of the field thought the foursome had forgotten what season it was, or simply believed they had literally "gone over the edge," is not clear. What's *crystal* clear, however, is that they mopped up most of the competition.

"I don't remember who won the tournament," he said, "but I know Mike and Bob, and Gary and Randy placed very high by fishing a pattern none of the rest of us knew about."

It turns out that the two teams had found an area where fine silt had built up along the bottom of a fairly steep break. And the walleyes were stacked up on the silt.

"I guess there was enough change in the bottom composition to attract the fish, or maybe there was some kind of insect hatch coming off the soft bottom," he said. "Either way, it's a pattern I'll never forget."

Reservoir walleyes, which typically spawn in tributary creeks, look for flats upon their return to the main part of the reservoir. "They'll head downstream, looking for flats near the river channel that offer warmer water and more forage," explains Glorvigen. "They could be tight to the shoreline in 8 or 9 feet of water, or on a secondary flat in 15 to 25 feet of water."

Side-scanning sonar could be the answer to finding walleyes in the shallow water, but in the deeper water, use your LCG, paper graph or flasher. "Secondary flats occur when the bottom drops gradually from the shoreline out to, say, 15 feet," he says. "From there to 25 feet the drop is *very* gradual (nearly flat). From 25 feet there's a pretty steep drop into the river channel. Walleyes will hold on that flat from 15 to 25 feet, relating to very subtle changes on the flat itself. All you have to do is motor along the breakline, keeping your eye on the screen. Any sort of bump, depression or anything else that's different from the bottom, will likely hold a walleye. If you see gamefish or baitfish, it's a bonus."

Early Summer

Early summer is when things start to bloom—vegetation is greening up and there is plenty of forage. And, forage is the key to finding walleyes on the expansive, shallow lakes. Focus your efforts on the weedbeds, especially those closest to the first major breakline. Depending on water clarity, weeds may stop growing in 6 feet of water (dirty water), or they could grow out to 18 feet (clear water), but the closer to the breakline they are, the more productive they'll be.

"A lot of presentations work now," Glorvigen says. "Bottom bouncers, jigs and floating live-bait rigs will all produce fish. Don't be afraid to fish right in the weeds. They'll be fairly sparse and you may be able to see walleyes and baitfish."

There's no trick to finding weeds on a sonar unit, but if there is confusion as to what's on the bottom, use the guide's simple technique. "Just tie on a heavy jig and throw it overboard," he says. "You'll be able to *feel* whether the bottom is soft or hard, and if weeds are there, try to hook one. If you take the time to physi-

Reservoir walleyes move toward downstream dams as summer progresses, then back upstream toward spawning areas in late summer and fall. Check main points, flats and structure near river channels.

Walleyes

cally find out what's on the bottom, you'll understand your sonar better, and you'll have more confidence in what it tells you the next time."

Early in the year, weedbeds are also a primary holding structure in deeper lakes, especially where there are points and pockets along the edges. Any sort of irregularity is bound to be more productive than a "wall" of weeds.

Reservoir walleyes can be found just about anywhere. Main points that stretch to the channel, deeper flats, saddles and coves and arms that contain decent weed growth are all potential hotspots. In one MWC tournament, the winner took his fish from a creek arm full of sunken tumbleweeds.

Summer

Sonar is a great asset when fishing the big, shallow lakes during the summer. One of the main hot-weather haunts are the expansive main-lake flats and, unless 20 other boats are already on the spot, a sonar unit equipped with loran or GPS is the key to finding them.

Rising normally 3 to 8 feet from the bottom, these giant flats will hold vast numbers of walleyes all summer long. When fish are active, they'll scatter over the top of the flat. Trolling bottom bouncers and covering lots of water will connect you with the most fish.

Much of the time, however, the walleyes are less active and tend to group a bit more tightly along the breakline into deeper water. You can often determine just how active or inactive they are, by noting how high up the slope they're located. Inactive fish tend to rest where the sloping edge meets the lake basin.

"I'll fish these walleyes with a Whistler jig and a piece of crawler, or a live-bait rig with a short leader," says Glorvigen. "You have to stay right on top of them with the sonar."

Other types of structure, such as rock reefs, sunken humps, points, fingers or any structural element that reaches into deep water becomes the focal point on dark, windy days. Such conditions cut light penetration, triggering the walleyes to move to the shallows to feed. With side-scanning sonar, you'll be able to pinpoint walleyes in these areas.

Deep natural lakes usually have many varied types of structure, and each will hold a certain population of walleyes. Weed-

Walleyes on a slightly sloping flat appear distinctly because of the paper graph's high resolution. Notice the tracings made by a jigging spoon as it traveled through the school. If the fish were more aggressive, they would be closer to the baitfish cloud in the upper right display. As it is, only one predator is visible, resembling an "ear" sticking out of the right side.

beds, breaklines, points and sunken humps are all classic walleye structure, and you should search them all until you find the most active fish. If you locate a school on a point, for example, but they aren't biting, move to another point or to a completely different type of structure. But, don't forget about the school you found. Go back from time to time to see if the fish have started feeding. Let the structure dictate your presentation. When fish are scattered, opt for trolling methods; use jigs if they're holding tightly to cover.

Walleyes in reservoirs can behave the same way. Some fish may be on breaklines, others may relate more to main points. "Check the main points first," says Glorvigen. "They're the primary summer structure." He begins searching at the first primary turn, then moves down the point.

Another option is to fish flats that run along the river channel. A typical cross-section would show the bottom sloping from the shoreline down to 35 feet, then gradually climbing to the top of the flat. It could be 2, 4, maybe even 8 or 10 feet higher. Depth remains fairly constant across the width of the flat, then the bottom drops quickly into the river channel. This calls for a quick-

Side-Scanning Units

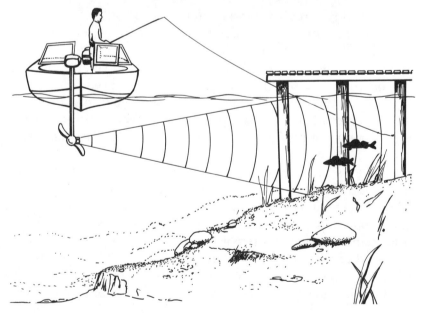

Side-scanning units are indispensable when looking for fish in shallow water. Cruising above the fish would spook and scatter them. The screen tells you their distance from the boat.

search method. Troll the length of the flat, searching with your sonar on top as well as on the breaks.

The important thing to remember about reservoir walleyes is that they migrate toward the dam (downriver) as the summer wears on, and away from the dam (upriver) when cooler weather prevails. So, if you can't find fish on a point where you had good luck the week before, head for the next large point that is closer to the dam.

Fall Fishing

The thing to remember when fishing during the fall, is that the general migration that just occurred through the summer simply reverses itself. Now the walleyes are moving from deeper, main-lake structure back to shallow structure, especially shallow

Reservoir Flats

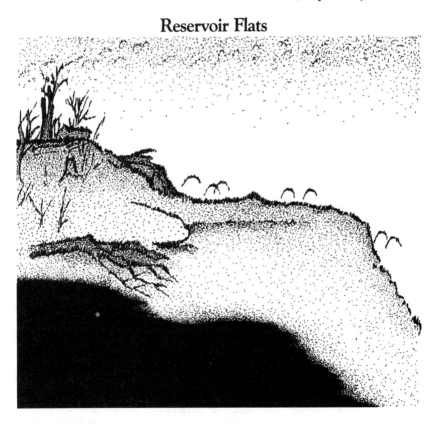

In reservoirs, flats near river basins hold walleyes all summer long. Look for subtle inconsistencies on the bottom that tend to attract and hold fish.

structure near spawning grounds.

Long, expansive points are often the main draw in the big, shallow lakes in the early fall—mid-August to September in northern states. From 7 to 12 feet of water is a good place to start your search, according to Glorvigen. Very often the fish are scattered on these points, so trolling would be the best technique.

In deeper lakes, classic structural elements (saddles, points, breaklines and weedbeds) close to shore will be most productive. And on reservoirs, walleyes will be on the move toward points, saddles and breaks that are farther "upstream."

Fall fishing sounds simple, and it is. Until turnover, that is. Once the surface water has cooled enough to sink to the depths, and water temperatures are fairly uniform throughout the water column, just about any spot in the lake is fair game to a walleye. Adequate oxygen levels in deep water make rocky humps likely spots. But, so are the shallows. Use what you've learned about sonar in scouring the entire lake until you find fish that are willing to cooperate. A spot any serious walleye angler will never pass up after the turnover is one that holds green weeds. They may be sparse, but they're almost certain to hold walleyes.

Open-Water Walleyes

Much has been learned over the years about where walleyes go and when. Top-notch anglers have devoted their lives to tracking walleye movements, and have done a great job of educating the rest of us. But, in the last few years, a walleye fishery that few anglers ever dreamed existed has been brought to the forefront. These are open-water walleyes—fish that relate to nothing but the available forage in vast expanses of water. The two pioneers in finding and catching these fish are Keith Kavajecz and Gary Parsons of Chilton, Wisconsin. The pair has been a driving force in both the MWC and PWT professional circuits.

"When we talk about open water," says Kavajecz, "we mean water over the main lake basin. The bottom is flat and featureless for miles and miles." The only reason those walleyes are there is because of the baitfish— whether they're alewives, smelt, yellow perch, shad or anything else.

What may be the most unique aspect of this type of fishing is that it relies solely on the use of electronic equipment, both sonar and navigational aids (loran and GPS), for success.

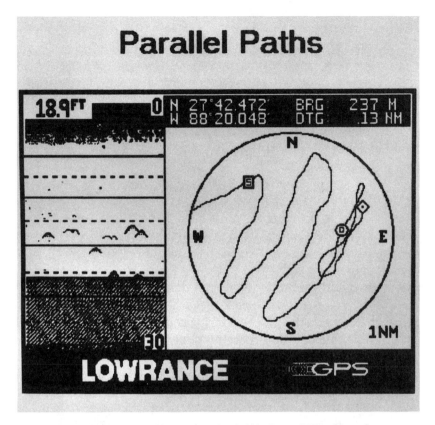

Parallel Paths

This is how a typical open-water trolling pattern would look on a GPS or loran plotter screen. Notice the spot where a fish was hooked and the trollers made several more passes.

Kavajecz and Parsons have used their open-water trolling techniques with great success in both the Great Lakes and inland lakes. Lake Erie, Lake Huron's Saginaw Bay and Lake Michigan's Little Bay de Noc have all given up impressive catches both in numbers and size, including a 13-plus-pounder that came from Bay de Noc.

"Our technique was originally developed as a summer method," says Kavajecz, "but in the last couple of years we've caught walleyes—big walleyes—in both the early spring and fall."

To find the fish, the pair uses a Lowrance LMS 300 LCG/loran unit. Both systems are an absolute must. The other requirement is that the loran unit be equipped with a plotter so you can see the boat's path on the screen. The combination unit is mounted on the console of their Skeeter 1850, a boat built for big water. It's also helpful to use a transducer that covers a wide swathe of water. The one they use shoots a 60-degree cone.

"The key is to go out and *look* for fish," Kavajecz explains. "Don't start fishing until you find them, or forage fish, on your screen." Because they deal with such a big area of water, even in a lake such as Wisconsin's Lake Winnebago, they had to develop a system that allows them to search as large an area as possible in a relatively short period of time. The system they came up with is called the skip-search.

"Once we get to where we want to fish," says Kavajecz, "we search with the sonar for about 100 yards, then run a quarter-mile. Then, we graph the bottom for 100 yards, and run another quarter-mile. Depending on the size of the body of water, the initial run may be a mile or five to six miles. We don't fish until we mark fish or baitfish."

Their LMS 300 has a split-screen feature that allows them to view both what the sonar is picking up as well as the loran plotter. So, as they travel, the plotter marks their path. When they come to the end of the first skip-search run, and they haven't found any walleyes, they can make a parallel run back down the lake a mile or so to either side of their original path, and do it accurately because they can see it on the screen.

The loran unit is also essential once they begin fishing. "When we start catching walleyes," Kavajecz says, "we can store waypoints along the trolling run. It gives us a reference to use throughout the day, as well as a target area to shoot for and utilize the next day."

As for trolling techniques, the pair seem to have a one-word vocabulary—*crankbaits*. Spring, summer or fall, they troll hard baits about 99 percent of the time—but not the *same* baits in each season.

"When water temperatures are 50 degrees or less, we go with subtle-action baits, like Jr. ThunderSticks or Rapalas. From 50 to 60 degrees, we fish moderate-action baits. Deep-diving ThunderSticks, Wally Divers and Shad Raps are a few examples. They have a bigger lip and a more active wobble. With temperatures above 60 degrees, we troll high-action baits, like Hot'N Tots, Wiggle Warts and Flat Warts."

Regarding color, the anglers stick with patterns based on chrome, silver and blue in the Great Lakes to mimic the important forage fish. On natural lakes, colors like orange and chartreuse get the nod because they represent yellow perch.

In setting the baits, the pair aims to cover a wide swathe, as well as the water column from top to bottom. Naturally, planer boards (for width) and lead-core line (for depth) come into play, especially in the summer.

"Walleyes can be at any depth in warm water," Kavajecz says, "and you need to cover the whole range with your lures. Even if your screen marks fish just off the bottom, remember that walleyes up near the surface will probably be spooked by the boat, and escape the sonar signal. Always run at least one bait in the 5- to 10-foot range."

The next time your summer hotspots, or for that matter, spring or fall structure, fail to produce, try the open water technique. Your partners will probably say that you're breaking the seasonal "rules." Just tell them that walleyes do, too.

=14=

Pike And Muskies

Visions of monster pike slashing an 8-inch spinner, or a huge muskie engulfing a foot-long jerkbait can, and usually will, send a trophy hunter who fishes for these massive predators into a daze. Eyes glaze over, hands and lips tremble and perspiration beads on the skin. Only after the whole scene has been played out, like a movie only he can see, will he snap out of the stupor. It can be dangerous for a pike fisherman to daydream.

The sad fact is, however, that most of the truly big pike and muskie catches are only a dream. Most anglers can fish for a lifetime without tying into a genuine trophy. Even the big-fish experts wade through a lot of small ones before they hang a brute.

This chapter is meant to help you use your sonar equipment to catch not only more, but bigger fish. Let's take a look at where muskies and pike generally hang out over the course of a season, and discuss when and how sonar will best serve you.

Early Season

While pike spawn earlier than muskies (normally when water temperatures reach the low to mid-40s for pike; 50 to 59 degrees for muskies), they tend to use the same type of shallow-bay areas. Many pike, in fact, travel farther back to spawn in marshes and tributaries adjacent to the bays.

Because both pike and muskies are protected while they are spawning by law in many states, we'll start with the open-season

Early in the season, pike can be found stacked in shallow water. Check local fishing regulations, however. In many states, pike are off limits during this time of year.

periods. Pike are eminently catchable during the period following the end of their spawning up to when the muskies move into the shallows. Look for them to go on a feeding rampage as the shallow water in the bays warms on bright, sunny days. Needless to say, this is not a situation where sonar will do you a lot of good. You will either be sight-fishing, or more likely, you'll catch fish by thoroughly combing the water with spoons and shallow-running crankbaits.

When the sky is gray, and the spring wind bites, pike will hang in deeper water just outside the bay, but they can be difficult to catch. Locate steep breaks near the mouth of the bay with your electronic equipment, then concentrate your sinking lures out away from the break. Occasionally, you'll be able to see these fish on your sonar screen.

Pike And Muskies

By the time muskies are ready to spawn, new weeds are starting to grow and new crops of baitfish emerge—both of which are keys to the coming fishing action.

Pete Maina, a Hayward, Wisconsin, muskie guide and four-time winner of Muskie Inc.'s national catch-and-release contest, loves more than anything to catch a 40-inch-plus 'lunge. He's not too bad on pike, either, having caught numerous fish of sizes that would please any angler. He runs a 17-foot Tuffy Esox, pushed by a 60-horsepower, tiller-controlled outboard. LCG units are strategically placed at both the rear and the front casting platforms.

Early in the season, after the spawn and the mandatory rest period occur, Maina finds muskies in new-growth weeds. "Look for the freshest, thickest weeds you can find near the spawning bays," he says. Depending on the water color, productive weed patches could be anywhere from 2 (dark water) to 12 (clear water) feet deep.

"Key on the places where structure changes," he explains. "Look for spots where the weeds change from one species to another, or where the weed growth thickens. Other productive spots might be those where a soft, weedy bottom turns to rock, or where weeds give way to submerged wood." Crankbaits and bucktail spinners are generally good baits at this time. But, remember that your presentation should put the lure right in the fish's face. You have to be able to adjust the presentation so that your lure touches the structure. "Twitch a crankbait as you retrieve it underwater," he says. "Run it right into the weed tops. It should hit the structure fairly frequently," he says.

In this case, sonar is an ally in locating structure; however, it's often in shallow enough water that you'll spook the fish as you motor over them. Find the weeds with your eyes, or with sonar if they're deeper (if you see baitfish, its all the better), mentally note the spot and return to it later.

One tip that Maina passes along deals with the weather conditions on the day you are fishing. Remember that water temperatures aren't all that high, so if you are fishing on an extremely warm spring day, take advantage of it. "If you notice that the water is warming fairly rapidly, switch to the biggest crank- or jerkbait you have," he says. "Muskies can get turned on in a hurry, and they'll be looking for big baitfish."

A new technological development can enhance your ability

Weeds And Crankbaits

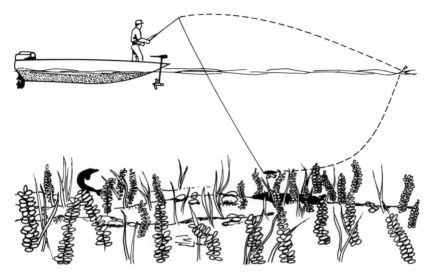

Shallow, weedy bays are great places to look for muskies and pike during early summer. Run your crankbait or spinner through the tops of plants to grab and hold your quarry's attention.

for this type of work, according to Maina. A new LCG from Bottom Line, called the Sidefinder, shoots a sonar beam horizontally from the boat. It tells you whether there are fish of at least 7 inches in length holding up to 120 feet from the transducer. "Even though the Sidefinder is designed specifically to locate fish, I still won't focus on finding muskies or pike," he says. "I look for bigger baitfish."

Summer Fishing

Summer is the time when everything in the lake is going full-bore. Water temperature is in the 70s, and vegetation is growing at a rapid rate. Baitfish, too, are plentiful. Consequently, it can be difficult to pinpoint where your game species may be holding, especially the bigger individuals in the population. Now's the time to regard the fishing method (locations as well as technique) you choose as a way to increase your chances of catching fish.

Weeds are still a key—but not just any weeds. Every angler has had the experience of fishing a good-looking bay or weed point, only to find that he can't keep 18-inch "hammer handles" off his hook. Granted, the odds of catching fish are incredibly

Weeds! You can bet that a good weedbed will hold pike. Lures that invade the vegetation will produce strikes.

high in such an area, but the chances of catching a fish of which to be proud are slim.

Weeds close to deeper water are what you're looking for in this situation. For muskies, main-lake structure, such as mid-lake bars and humps become more important as well, according to Maina.

"My favorite is an offshore rock bar that comes out of a muck bottom and tops out at 15 to 20 feet," he says. Wind velocity and water clarity (which together or separately dictate light penetration) play an important role. Dirty water or strong winds could mean that shallower bars may be the ticket to finding big fish. Cast or troll big crankbaits or weighted spinners around the edges of such structure.

Good sonar equipment is a must when fishing rock bars. Again, don't be caught up with the idea that you need to actually *see* fish on the screen. Look instead for the fish-holding structure. If it's a rock bar you seek, use the grayline feature on an LCG, or watch how the signal strength changes on a flasher dial, to identify spots where the bottom changes from soft to hard.

When fishing weedlines, concentrate on those that are near deeper water, like a weedbed that grows out to the first major breakline. Then, focus your fishing on the deep edge. Casting lures is probably the most popular technique; however, in this case, trolling is a good alternative.

All edges aren't created equal, either. Those with a lot of points, pockets and turns will be more attractive to fish than those that look like a solid "wall" of vegetation. Use your sonar to locate it, then identify what type of weedbed you're dealing with.

On lakes with less light penetration, weeds often won't grow all the way out to the breakline. Big pike don't like to cross the weedless space to get to cover, so try finding them on the structure on the break itself. Trolling may be the best bet.

If the typical summer hotspots don't pay off, Maina suggests taking a shot at suspended fish. "Keep an eye on the thermocline," he says, "and pay special attention to bars that top out just above the thermocline." As a brief refresher, the thermocline is a band of water—rapidly decreasing in temperature from top to bottom—that sets up in lakes, stratifying into temperature zones in the summer. It will show up on your sonar screen as a light-gray shadow if you increase the gain setting on your unit.

Some days, muskies will lie just above the thermocline, while

This is a pike hunter's dream come true. Knowledge of the quarry, combined with good sonar skills will lead to close encounters with trophy fish.

pike dip below it from time to time. This is when you should be looking for fish on the screen, especially baitfish, according to Maina. "Look for schools of baitfish," he says. "They may be panfish, small walleyes, ciscoes or any other species, but key on them."

Late Summer To Fall

As summer winds down, daylight hours grow noticeably shorter and water temperatures begin to drop. When they drop from the summer's peak temperature (generally about 78 degrees) to around 70 degrees, big fish are vulnerable. In fact Maina says, "This is the best time of year to catch a big muskie on artificial lures: bucktail spinners, crankbaits and jerkbaits. The fish start migrating back toward the shallows, and they are very catchable."

Weed edges, especially the edges of late-growing weeds like coontail, are areas on which to concentrate. Spots that produced fish in the early part of the season should be good again. They may be weeds on flats, or weeds that form a point. Either way, they must have easy access to deep water to be attractive to big fish. Again, side-scanning sonar can be used to pinpoint baitfish in likely areas.

Don't be afraid to explore areas that you think are *too* shallow, he adds. The point was driven home to him by accident during a late-August fishing trip with a pair of clients. "I had the boat positioned so that we could cast toward a weed edge that was in 4 to 5 feet of water," he says. "Somehow I let the boat get out of position, and before I realized that we were sitting directly over the spot I wanted to be casting *to*, I shot a cast toward shore."

The bucktail landed in approximately 2 feet of water; however, less than 6 feet into the retrieve a 15-pound muskie attacked the lure. "Some people just don't realize how shallow these fish can be," he says.

When fall weather comes into full swing, waters cool to the point where stratified lakes turn over. That is, surface water cools and drops to the bottom. The thermocline disappears and water temperatures become more uniform from top to bottom.

Pike anglers can stay on the weed edges, casting crankbaits, or if the fish are less active, long rubber lizards on jig heads up to 1 ounce. Muskies and some pike, however, move to other areas. Maina likes to look for muskies along sharp breaklines that head

Big rubber-body baits on heavy jig heads are very effective when fishing for muskies and pike, especially during the fall season.

into deeper water. Check those sharp-breaking spots near the summer-holding areas first. You'll be able to see fish, and baitfish, on the sonar screen. Trolling deep-diving crankbaits or crankbaits and bucktails on downriggers will do the trick.

One other pattern worth mentioning occurs as water temperatures approach 40 degrees on lakes that hold ciscoes. These oily forage fish spawn in the fall on sandy flats. You can see them easily on your sonar screen, says Maina, as they move from the main lake in near the shallow spawning beds.

"When you find a school of ciscoes in the 25- to 30-foot range, muskies will position themselves on the lake side of the school," he says. "As they move toward shallower water, the predators move closer to the school. Finally, when the ciscoes approach the primary breakline, the muskies will skirt the school, move up onto the flats and attack the school from the shallows."

Deep, hard-bottom areas attract muskies after the water cools further. Maina suggests using sonar to identify these areas and trolling deep-diving crankbaits (downriggers are also helpful), or fishing live or dead bait on quick-set rigs.

Whether pike or muskies are your target, remember there will be times that sonar will be of great help to you; other times you'll have to rely on your own knowledge of the lake. Either way, a good lake map is essential. No serious angler would venture onto the water without one.

15

Trout And Salmon

P ulling into the parking lot of a Lake Michigan public ac-cess in Ludington, Michigan, an angling pair noticed that the only visible sign of an approaching car ferry was a smudge of black smoke on the horizon. It was a mid-August evening with a light breeze coming in off the big lake.

Although they were novices at the Great Lakes trolling game, they knew the salmon were staging just offshore in preparation for the fall spawning run, and were confident that their 16-foot alu-minum boat could get them to where the big kings swam. They stowed gear and prepared downriggers as they motored through the mouth of the Pere Marquette River and into open water. They didn't even glance at the sonar unit until they were 50 yards be-yond the pierheads. They pointed the bow toward a group of big trolling boats about a mile out, and noticed again the car ferry coming from Kewaunee, Wisconsin. They could see the whole ship, its stacks protruding well above the line where the sky met the water.

About that time one of the anglers also noticed some activity happening on the pier. The group of anglers that had been spread out casting Little Cleo spoons was now huddled together watch-ing one fisherman. This attention-getting pier fisherman, who had been casting into the channel earlier, was now trying to con-trol whatever was making his 9-foot spinning rod buck like a bronco. The excitement was building with each counter-attack he made. While he was fighting this monstrous fish, another ang-

King salmon haunting deep waters in the Great Lakes can be difficult to find. A sophisticated trolling rig, complete with mast and planer boards, will help get the job done.

Trout And Salmon   199

ler helped him by grabbing the landing net and filling the basket with a big king. What's more, still another angler was straining against an arched rod. The action was incredible!

After setting the downriggers, they started trolling back the way they had come. For 15 minutes, they scoured the waters between the pierheads without a knock-off, even though you could see small groups of baitfish on the flasher dial. Worse still, the pier anglers each landed another fish.

Unable to stand it any more, they decided to troll as close as possible to the end of the south pier. Almost instantly, the flasher lit up with baitfish. Still, the first pass didn't produce a hit. Nor did the second. Something was wrong, but they didn't know what. Out of desperation, they dropped one cannonball about 4 feet, trying to make it run beneath the baitfish. Nothing. Next, they jerked a line and quickly replaced the spoon with one about half its size. Bingo!

The knock-off was violent, and was followed by a long, burning run. It took several minutes to gain back all of the 65 yards of 12-pound monofilament. When they finally did, they had a sleek, strong 26-pound king flopping on the deck.

Their clumsy attempts to quickly reset the downriggers and turn the boat were interrupted by a long blast from an air horn that lifted both of them clear of the swivel seats. Somehow that car ferry, packed full of railroad cars, automobiles and passengers, had cruised to within a quarter-mile and was closing fast.

That one king ended up being their last. Less than a minute after the ship passed between the pierheads, a flock of seagulls descended to the surface and began gobbling dead and stunned alewives. The salmon had cleared out, as well.

Although their fishing success was short-lived, the incident taught two valuable lessons. First, *never* ignore your sonar for more than a few seconds at a time. If they had paid attention to the flasher, they might have seen the baitfish and probably would have caught several salmon before the car ferry disrupted the feeding spree. Second, always remember how finicky salmon can be when making your lure selection—size matters.

Another lesson learned is the value of a quality LCG when fishing the big lakes. A flasher alone, although good enough to penetrate to 60 feet, won't pick up salmon in their deep, summer haunts. "High-quality sonar equipment is a must for big-lake troll-

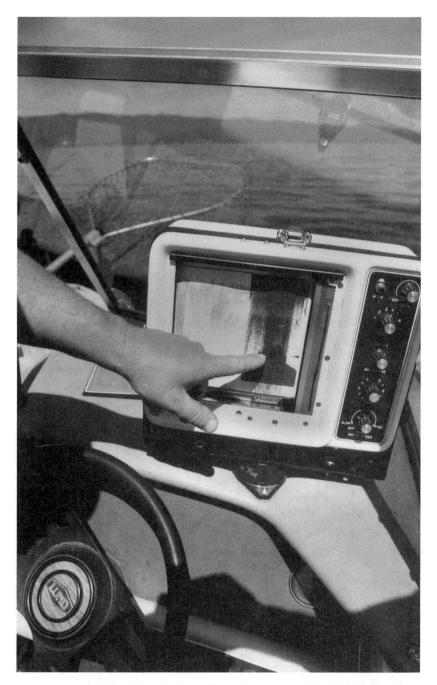

A giant cloud of baitfish blacks out a good portion of this paper graph display. Even if you don't see "hooks" made by hungry trout or salmon, it's a good idea to run your lure through it.

Trout And Salmon 201

ing," says charter captain Bob Cinelli, who runs both a Raytheon video unit and a Lowrance LMS 300 sonar/loran unit on his Lake Ontario charter boat. With help from his electronics, he boats more than 1,500 salmon and trout per year for the anglers who hire Cinelli's Sport Fishing Service.

Quality sonar equipment is critical in order to find baitfish, gamefish and mid-lake structure that, during the summer, is often 150-plus feet below the surface. Mid-lake structure—on the Great Lakes? Yes, just like any other fish, big-lake salmon and trout must relate to something, and, that something is usually an edge where cool water meets warm water. But, we're jumping too far ahead. Let's look at a typical season and follow the patterns as the season progresses.

Early Spring

Depending on the year, Great Lakes trollers typically hit the water in a serious fashion in March or April. The water is cold, and fishing is concentrated along the shallows. Sunlight heats the shallow shoreline shelves, warming the water and causing micro-organisms in the water to begin multiplying. Baitfish are drawn to the food source, and they are followed by the gamefish.

Smelt-imitating plugs, such as Rapalas, Bomber Long-A's and Rebel Fastracs, are fished on flatlines and planer boards in water generally 5 to 15 feet deep. "Salmon could be spread anywhere along the shoreline," says Cinelli. "The key you're looking for is water above 39 degrees in temperature."

A surface temperature gauge is the primary electronic tool you rely on at this time of year. Your sonar gear simply keeps you off the bottom. "When you're fishing in 6 feet of water and your boat drafts 38 inches, it only takes one big rock to get you into a lot of trouble," says Cinelli.

Late Spring

From late April to June, however, trolling efforts move to deeper water, and focus more on bottom structure and the presence of baitfish rather than a temperature edge. At Olcott, important areas are small stair-step breaks and other subtle differences in bottom structure in water that is approximately 100 feet deep. If baitfish are present, the spot is as good as gold, according to Cinelli.

When you see this result from your unit, you know you're in business for some exciting and rewarding fishing action.

"Alewives come into play for the first time of the season," he says. If you find the structure, and see baitfish on your screen, you *know* the salmon will show up sooner or later. Typically, the alewives form large horizontal rafts that are sometimes many feet thick and stretch for up to a mile. The trick is to troll just outside the raft so your lures don't get "lost" in the mass of forage.

This is when Cinelli packs away his body baits and breaks out the trolling spoons: lightweight metal strips perfect for running behind cannonballs. "It's not that body baits won't work this time of year," he says. "The problem is that they sometimes work against you. They give big fish more leverage to tear free of the hooks. You can modify them somewhat by removing all but the rear set of trebles, but I'd much rather catch a big salmon on a spoon. I'm more confident it will stay hooked."

Some big-lake trollers mount their electronic gear on the boat's stern. This is where the majority of the action takes place.

Summer

When summer fully blooms, salmon and trout stratify in the water column, according to their preferred temperature ranges. Steelhead, for example, generally cruise the warmer surface waters, while salmon seek out cooler water below. Lake trout prefer even lower temperatures, and either mingle with the salmon, or hold even deeper.

"Summer fishing takes place even farther offshore," says Cinelli. "I look for them in water 150 to 600 feet deep."

Again, edges are the key factor, and your temperature gauge is just as important as your sonar equipment. Out in deep water, look for edges on your screen. What you'll see might be the thermocline, an area where waters of two different temperatures meet, or upwellings and current sheers where waters are moving in two different directions. It's easy to see a big ball of alewives on the screen; however, the edge is another matter. "They look like a shadowy gray line," says Cinelli, "almost like a false bottom reading."

Often, the thermocline is depicted in drawings that accompany fishing articles as being arrow-straight, and at one level

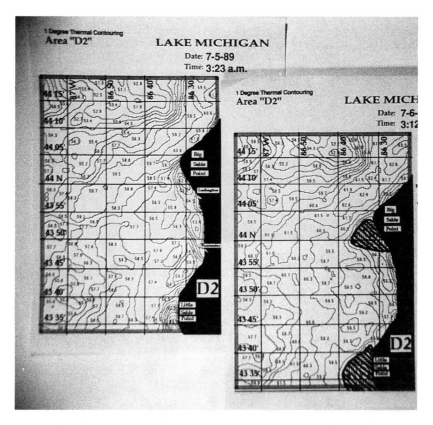

Water temperature is so critical in trout and salmon fishing on the big lakes that some skippers subscribe to a service that feeds them updated thermal contours via facsimile machine.

throughout the lake. In truth, it goes up and down in reaction to natural water movements caused by sub-surface currents or wind and wave action. Thus, a productive edge may be more vertical than horizontal.

"Upwellings and current sheers are places where, for some reason, lots of microorganisms collect," he explains. "Baitfish move in to eat the microscopic food, and the predators concentrate on the baitfish."

Rather than skirting the edges of a pod of baitfish, as he does earlier in the year, Cinelli's summer trolling presentation is much more aggressive. "Now baitfish balls are smaller and more compact. You blow right through the alewives, trying to create a little activity that will attract gamefish," he says. "You want the rodtips to rattle as baitfish bounce off your monofilament line."

Trout And Salmon

Another edge occurs where river currents flow into the main lake. In Cinelli's area, it's the Niagara River, which dumps extremely warm Lake Erie water into Lake Ontario, creating current edges that attract both bait- and gamefish.

Wind direction and strength affect which way river currents flow once they enter a big lake. Experience, and possibly other more knowledgeable anglers, will tell you how the wind affects the river current in your area. Where Cinelli fishes, anglers prefer a good south wind. "Wind from the south pushes the current north, straight out into the lake and creates cooler upwellings closer to the southern shore," he explains. "You'll have good, fishable water just a mile or two from the harbor."

By contrast, winds from the north stack warm river water along the southern shore, building an expansive area of water that's too warm for the salmon. The fish hang farther out in deeper, cooler water, and anglers must follow them.

Late Summer

About the second or third week of August, Great Lakes salmon start moving back toward shallow water, staying there until all the right environmental factors come together to trigger a migration up spawning streams. They feed heavily, putting on fat that will be burned off a few weeks later during the migration. "They're back in water approximately 80 to 100 feet deep," says Cinelli, "and relating to the same sort of subtle structure they did during late spring."

Stair-step breaks and small depressions or bumps on the bottom seem to attract the fish, as do baitfish. As you did earlier in the season, look for structure and alewives with your sonar equipment. When you find the two together, hang on to the rod!

Spoons work on late-summer salmon, but Cinelli often opts for a dodger and squid when the water starts to cool. The big, lazy-looking attractor seems to lure bigger fish, and the soft, rubber artificial squid, which yields easily under pressure, seldom lets them escape. "I probably enjoy fishing a dodger-and-squid combination more than any other bait," says Cinelli. "There's nothing more satisfying than a dodger-and-squid flurry."

He's referring to a phenomenon that seems to occur on a consistent basis when fishing these baits. "The typical scenario is that while one of your anglers is fighting a fish, you can see on the so-

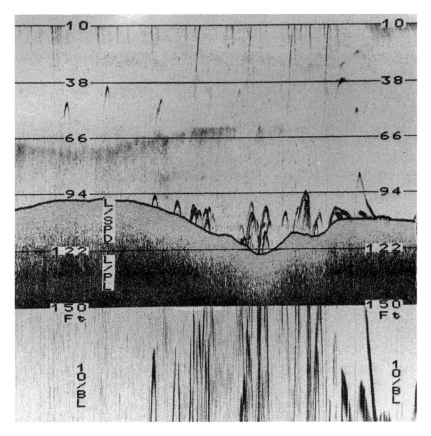

These hooks on the bottom, in 100 feet of water, are most likely some good-sized lake trout.

nar that several more have moved into your lures. It seems that the first fish to hit will often trigger others to become aggressive, and you'll often end up with multiple hookups."

The salmon's next step is to run up the river to spawn, literally bringing the open-water season for adult fish to a close for the year. Juvenile salmon are still available in the lake, but Cinelli strongly urges anglers to leave them for the next year. "Those are 3-year-old fish," he says, "and if everybody concentrated on them, where would next year's fish come from. When the spawning run is over, it's time to put the boat away for the winter."

Final Thoughts

Trolling lore varies in different areas of the Great Lakes. Indeed, there are few things that individual anglers agree on completely. But the fact is, it's not necessary that every angler conform to some mold. Whatever the angler does, and however he does it, should fulfill no other goal than to allow him to enjoy his fishing as much as possible.

With that in mind, however, a few points that Cinelli brings up are worth examining. Whether or not you agree with them is your option.

The first deals with choosing a sonar unit. "Don't skimp when shopping for a sonar unit," he says. "Always purchase the best you can afford. Decide how much you are willing to spend, then look around for a unit with the highest power and best resolution. Also, make sure it can be easily serviced."

After you make the purchase, be sure to follow installation instructions carefully. "Each unit comes with a manual that shows you exactly how to install it in your boat. I can't stress enough that it's important to read the book carefully and follow its instructions. Most of the trouble people have with their equipment stems from faulty installation."

Cinelli is just as particular about how the transducer is mounted. "When attaching the transducer," he says, "be sure to use the manual provided. It will suggest mounting options for different types of hulls. Each hull is different, and transducers should be custom-mounted to the hull. Again, read the manual and follow the directions carefully. That way, you'll get the best performance possible."

Many anglers choose to mount the puck so that it points into the water behind the boat. They want to see their cannonballs (and approaching gamefish) on the screen. Cinelli prefers to use a through-the-hull transducer that sends the signal straight down. With its 60-degree cone angle, he can see what's in front of the boat as well as anything approaching his lures. "I'm also convinced that a through-the-hull transducer is the only way to go on a larger, inboard power boat. It allows you more versatility. I can get a better reading at high speeds because there is no interference from prop wash."

Cinelli also has definite ideas about lure placement. While some anglers simply set their artificials at the depth where most of the salmon seem to be, he arranges his baits in a precise pattern. Some cannonballs run higher; some lower. Some lures have a short lead; others a long lead. That arrangement, along with other

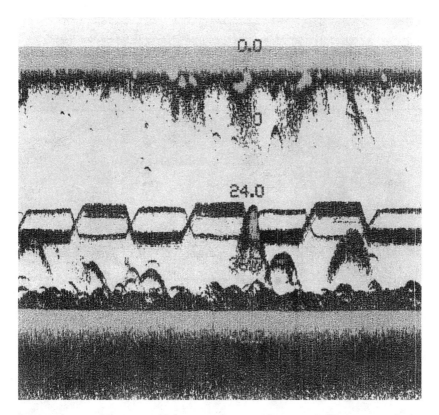

Set properly, a good sonar unit will show you where your downrigger balls are running. In this case, a pair of them alternately oscillate from two automatic downrigger units. Studying patterns is extremely important for fishing success.

factors, come together into what Cinelli calls a *trolling program.*

"I think that, on any particular day, fish will be triggered by a certain bait, moving in a certain way at a certain speed," he says. "If you don't know what those factors are, you must vary your approach. Some of the lures serve as attractors, bringing fish close enough to zero-in on a particular one. After awhile, you'll be able to pinpoint the most productive pattern and focus on that one. If the action stops, you go back to the program, and try to determine which setup will trigger a strike next.

"Start with your high-percentage baits first," he adds, "the ones you have the most confidence in. But, if you don't get action right away, don't panic, either. Don't switch the baits too quickly. Sometimes it's necessary to work the fish over in order to get the strike."

When everything comes together, the result is a trophy fish like this one. Practice and hands-on experience with sonar are your best bet.

Complete Angler's Library

Lure color, according to Cinelli, is a bit more difficult to pin down. A good portion of his 5,000 spoons are plain silver plates or black-and-white ones. He'd rather choose a certain spoon for its running qualities, and then color it with one or more pieces of colored prism tape. "I have to find out what exactly will trigger a fish on a certain day. The tape allows me to experiment to a greater degree than if I had to rely only on colored lures."

Coming up with tape patterns is serious business around Olcott, according to Cinelli. "It's like a fly tier creating the perfect dry fly," he says. "You have to be very conscious of the details. It's a real science, and the best part about it is that any angler on the water is capable of coming up with a hot combination."

Returning To
That Spot

16

The Advantages Of Loran, GPS

Sonar units—LCGs, paper graphs and flashers—are the angler's underwater eyes. But, what about above the surface? True, many times you simply know from experience that the hump you're looking for is just 60 yards off that point and lined up with the cottonwood tree on the shoreline and the high-voltage electrical tower on the hill. Other times, however, the structure you seek may be miles from shore, with no way to visibly triangulate its position.

That's when you need the assistance of another type of marine electronic device, one that can put you back onto that hotspot you found the day before. For years, loran (LOng RAnge Navigation) has been the way to do it. New to the fishing scene, however, is the Global Positioning System (GPS), which many believe will make the loran system obsolete in a few years.

Both were developed as aids to navigation, first for the military, then for commercial use. Innovative electronic engineers, however, developed receivers for the sportfishing market that allow everyday anglers to take advantage of high-tech government resources. In this chapter, we'll take a look at both systems, and discuss how each one works.

Loran-C
Loran-C is second-generation technology. The first was loran-A, which was developed during World War II and used initially by the U.S. Coast Guard. Later, loran-A was opened to commer-

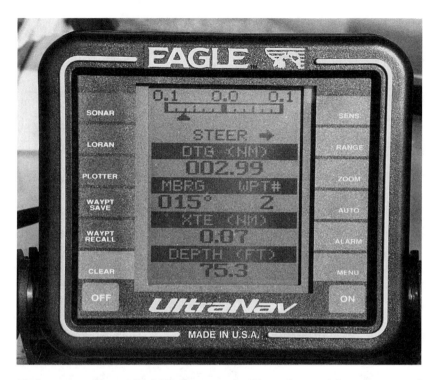

The loran system has served faithfully for many years. This unit's screen helps you steer toward a waypoint. The indicator at the top tells you how far off course you are and the steer message with arrow tells you how to get back on course. DTG means the remaining distance to the waypoint in nautical miles. MBRG is the magnetic or compass heading to the waypoint, and WPT# tells you which waypoint from the unit's memory you're approaching. XTE is cross-track error; the distance in nautical miles that you're off course.

cial use. Loran-C is simply a more accurate version of its predecessor.

The loran system consists of a series of land-based radio transmitting towers located around the world that are electronically linked into "chains" that contain three to five transmitters, or stations. Each chain covers a certain geographic region.

Each station transmits specifically timed signals around the clock. When you turn on your loran receiver, it locks onto the signals from at least three stations in the chain, and automatically designates one to be the master signal. The rest are assigned secondary roles. By calculating the slight difference in time it takes for each signal to reach your antenna (usually an 8-foot whip), the receiver can pinpoint its location in latitude and longitude within about 100 feet of the true spot. Accuracy depends on a number of

The Loran System

The loran system uses radio waves from transmitters that are hundreds of miles apart in order to triangulate your position.

Complete Angler's Library

factors that will be covered later.

How does loran help fishermen? Really, the answer lies with the creativity of the operator. Generally, though, it functions as a tool to get you from one spot to another, whether it be an offshore hotspot, or a safe harbor when heading home through a fog bank. As mentioned, the receiver determines its position and displays the information in latitude and longitude readings on the screen. If the spot is one to which you want to return, simply press a button and it is stored as a waypoint in the unit's memory. A day, week or year later, you can return to that spot from anywhere on that body of water simply by recalling the waypoint. The unit will give you a compass reading, steering instructions and tell you how far away the desired position is from where you sit. Some units can show you a "picture" of your boat on a plotter display, revealing your path of travel and whether you're remaining on course or sliding off.

You can even pass along the latitude and longitude readings to a friend. He simply punches them into his unit and can fish the same spot where you caught fish the day before. Accuracy will be a little less precise, however, because the information was obtained on another unit.

Creativity with loran comes with experience. Probably the most shining example is what Keith Kavajecz and Gary Parsons, a pair of master walleye anglers and top-notch sonar operators, discovered they could do with their loran unit. The technique that they call "Etch-A-Sketching" has been described fully in *North American Fisherman*. Briefly, however, the duo uses their loran unit to plot structure and outline trolling patterns on their display screen. For example, on a mid-lake mudflat, they will motor slowly around the edge of the flat, using their sonar equipment to keep them as close to on top of the breakline as possible. All the while, their loran plotter "draws a map" of the flat.

Once complete, the pair has a visual reference on the screen of what's underneath the surface. More importantly, it's one that also shows their boat position, wherever it may be. When they start trolling, the plotter draws the path of travel, and the anglers can see exactly where in relation to the flat their baits have been. They fish more efficiently, never covering the same water twice unless it's to return to a spot where they just picked up a fish. All in all, their success rate increased dramatically with this system.

Some sonar units provide the option of adding loran capabilities. This unit has a split-screen feature that allows you to use your sonar and navigate at the same time!

Global Positioning System

GPS serves the same purpose as loran, namely to show you where you are and the best way to get to where you want to go. Unlike loran, though, its central nervous system is based in space. Twenty-four satellites, 21 operational and three spares, will be orbiting the earth and sending signals to receivers on the surface. By 1992, there were 16 satellites in orbit, which were being used on a regular basis by the military and others. With the completion of the launch schedule, there would be four satellites in each of six orbits. Each satellite makes two trips around the earth during each 24-hour period.

Actually a wonder of technology, each solar-powered satellite contains an atomic clock, which is accurate to within one second every 300,000 years. The satellites continuously broadcast the time and their locations in space.

On earth, a GPS receiver locks onto signals from at least three satellites (some can listen to five satellite signals at a time). The receiver calculates its position by measuring the interval between the time the signal was transmitted and when it was received. With signals from three satellites, it can pinpoint its latitude and longitude location; with four signals, it can also determine its altitude.

Like the loran system, GPS can steer you to a new waypoint, either with steering instructions or by a diagram on a plotting screen, depending on which unit you use. Its accuracy has been highly acclaimed. Some early field-testers say they've returned to within just a few feet of a waypoint they had previously stored in the receiver's memory.

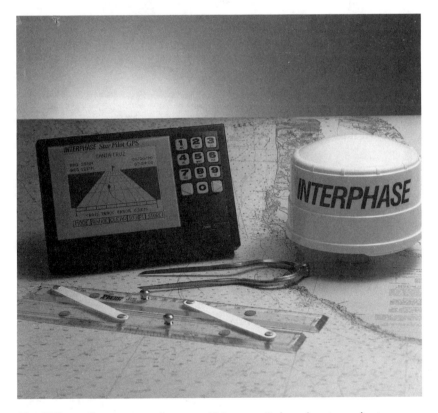

This GPS unit offers superior performance with its proven 3-channel receiver and unique, easy-to-understand graphic displays. It features large digital readouts, track plotting and cross track error displays. (Notice the antenna at right.)

The Global Positioning System

A total of 24 GPS satellites, including three spares, make up the system. Signals are not affected by bad weather or interference.

Accuracy, however, can be variable with GPS. That's because there are actually two signals sent from each satellite. One is called the "precise signal" (P-code), which allows a receiver to consistently pinpoint its position within a foot or two. The P-code is reserved for military use only. For worldwide civilian use, the course-acquisition signal (C/A-code) is used. Manufacturers generally claim the C/A-code is accurate to about 80 feet. But, because of something called "selective availability" (SA) interference by the United States Department of Defense (DOD), accuracy of civilian units can be severely downgraded.

At its discretion, the DOD can engage SA, which inserts random errors into the information transmitted by the satellites. The purpose is to maintain the system's military effectiveness. In other words, the government doesn't want military-grade GPS units to

Hand-held units were among the first GPS products commercially available. Lightweight and portable, they served not only anglers, but hunters, hikers, foresters, surveyors and many others.

be sold in sporting goods stores and outdoor sports catalogs.

SA can be engaged at the government's will, and it also can vary the extent to which the C/A-code is manipulated. Numerous field tests of civilian GPS units have shown extremely high accuracy rates, however, leaving testers to conclude that the SA function was not engaged at the time. Experts and field-testers alike are quick to agree that potential GPS users shouldn't be frightened by the SA factor, as it is a tool designed to be used in times of national emergency.

While it would be difficult and expensive for the average GPS user to adopt the technique, "differential GPS" (DGPS) is a way to overcome SA interference. It requires one GPS unit to be placed at a known location, and the information from that receiver is used to adjust the readings of remote receivers. In fact, plans call for DGPS units to be installed at all the major airports to maintain air-traffic-control capabilities.

Even if you're not ready for GPS in your fishing boat right now, you can be sure the technology will touch your life at sometime in the future. There's a raft of professionals, from surveyors to archaeologists, already using GPS. Furthermore, it's predicted that someday GPS receivers may be as common as the telephone. Futurists say, for example, that every modern automobile will be

The Advantages Of Loran, GPS   221 equipped with GPS, making trip-planning and route-selection as easy as pushing a button.

GPS Vs. Loran

Understandably, there is much difference of opinion about whether GPS will reign over loran. The facts are that, at the moment, no one knows for sure. GPS, according to the experts, holds many advantages, but for now, loran still has an ace-in-the-hole—namely, price. While the best loran units are available for a few hundred dollars, GPS units were introduced at about $1,000 each. *Big* money for a fishing tool.

Still, there will be a lot of people who'll buy at that price. Others will wait until retail prices drop, as they usually do with new electronic devices. Others still, will go on contentedly with their loran units. The question is, "how many anglers will fall into each category, especially the latter two?"

To decide for yourself, you need to know how they stack up against one another, and determine if the benefits offered by GPS are worth the money for the type of fishing you do.

• *Speed And Accuracy.* It's generally accepted that GPS, even with the SA factor, is more accurate than loran. It can put you more closely over a precise spot. Moreover, the GPS plotter display can be set to represent only one-twentieth of a nautical mile, compared to about a quarter-mile on a loran plotter, so the detail is much greater. GPS also processes information faster than loran does. For instance, with a loran unit, it may take several seconds for a course direction change to show up on the plotter. The lag-time for GPS is only about a second.

As one GPS technician who mounted a unit on his automobile said, "From a dead stop, I could only get about half way through an intersection before I could see my car's movement on the screen."

• *Ease Of Operation.* GPS manufacturers tout the unit's operating ease, "simply turn it on and go." It's true, too. Requiring only about 30 seconds to acquire the satellite signals and set itself, the GPS receiver has loran's one- to three-minute set-up time beat. Once in use, GPS is pretty much automatic, as well. Loran often requires a bit of fine-tuning by the operator.

The antenna required by GPS vs. loran may also be an overlooked factor until you get onto the water. How often have you

GPS Vs. Loran

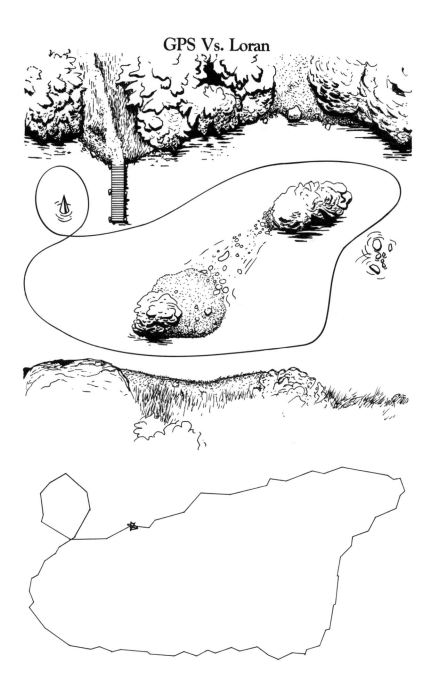

A side-by-side comparison of GPS and loran may help you get a better understanding of their differences. Here, the map of a specific course is shown (top); and, one lap around the course with GPS (bottom).

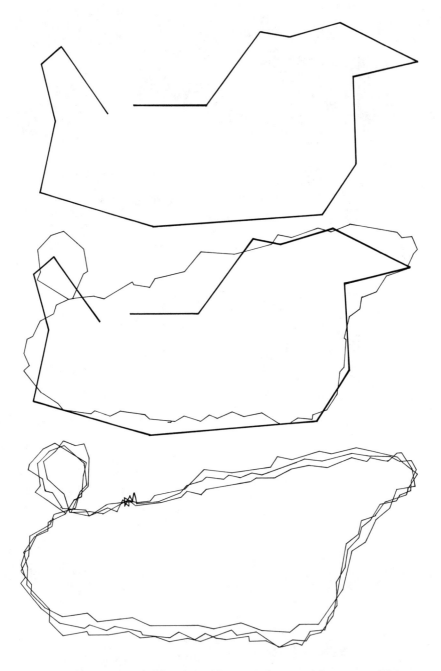

Continuing with the comparison of GPS and loran, one lap around the course with loran is shown (top). GPS and loran together may show a more vivid difference (middle). Finally, three laps around the course with only GPS is illustrated.

hooked the loran's whip antenna on the backcast? Maybe it's only a nuisance when you're fighting a fish. With the low-profile GPS antenna, both problems disappear.

Because the transmission source is in space, the GPS antenna can be short (only a few inches from the surface it's mounted on) and flat. Loran antennae must be tall to catch the transmissions flowing along the earth's surface.

● *Interference.* Probably the biggest advantage GPS has over loran is that its function is unaffected by interference caused by bad weather, or other electronic sources. Thunderstorms, cold fronts, strong signals from other transmitters and sometimes interference from other electronic devices on the boat can play havoc with loran. GPS seems to be immune to these types of situations and problems.

Antennae: Loran Vs. GPS

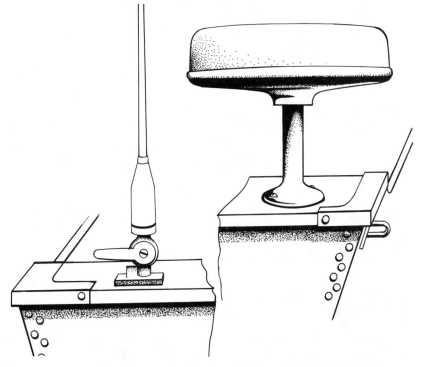

Loran antennae must be tall (average length is about 8 feet) to catch earth's land-based transmissions. They are usually mounted toward the back of the boat (left). GPS antennae can be fairly short (average length is about 1.5 to 2 feet), because they catch transmissions from space satellites. They are also mounted toward the back of the boat (right).

Stormy weather (such as this), as well as other electronic sources, can cause interference problems for the loran system. In comparison, the global positioning system would not be affected.

Complete Angler's Library

Which Is For You?

In the face of the comparison we've just made, the choice seems obvious. But is it, really? While many manufacturers and a few anglers say GPS is superior, none of them stamps loran as a bad system. It's been used successfully for years, and a long future is virtually assured. The government has reportedly vowed to maintain the loran system well into the next century.

So how do you choose? Simply look at the type of fishing you do most. Maybe you're a structure fisherman who probes every nook and cranny of a submerged hump, and GPS would save you an hour a day search-time. Perhaps you only use a navigation aid to get to a general area and back again. And you rely more on sonar for information. Loran is probably your choice.

It boils down to what works best for *you*. Whichever system, if any, brings you the most enjoyment during your time on the water is the one for you.

Index